PASSION & FIRE

PASSION & FIRE

IGNITING YOUR PASSION FOR GOD

NATHAN SHAW
Foreword by John L. Sandford

Passion and Fire
Published by Castle Publishing Ltd
New Zealand

www.castlepublishing.co.nz

© 2007 & 2013 Nathan Shaw

ISBN 978-0-9582822-1-5 (Softcover)
ISBN 978-0-9876682-2-6 (ePUB)
ISBN 978-0-9876682-3-3 (Kindle)

Editing & Production: Andrew Killick
Cover design: Jeff Hagan
Cover image: Big Stock Photo

Scripture taken from the New King James Version.
Copyright © 1982 by Thomas Nelson, Inc.
Used by permission. All rights reserved.

Scripture quotations marked AMP are taken from
the Amplified® Bible, Copyright © 1954, 1958, 1962, 1964, 1965, 1987
by The Lockman Foundation
Used by permission. (www.Lockman.org)

Scripture quotations marked NLT are taken from
the Holy Bible, New Living Translation, copyright 1996, 2004.
Used by permission of Tyndale House Publishers, Inc.,
Wheaton, Illinois 60189. All rights reserved.

ALL RIGHTS RESERVED

No part of this publication may be reproduced,
stored in a retrieval system, or transmitted
in any form or by any means, electronic, mechanical,
photocopying, recording or otherwise,
without prior written permission from the author or publisher.

To Jill Austin,

As a teenager I yearned to know God intimately and experientially. My desperate cry was answered and my heart set on fire through your ministry. Thank you for embracing the passion of God's heart and burning with the blazing fire of His love.

I am eternally grateful.

There is no greater pleasure than knowing that we are loved passionately by a merciful and kind God and that because of this we can freely and willingly pour our lives out in holy abandonment to Him. Nathan's book *Passion and Fire*, calls us into the knowledge of this reality. It will awaken and stir the hearts of all who read it.

Mike Bickle, Author, Director of International House of Prayer, Kansas City. www.fotb.com

Superficiality seems to characterise most of the relationships we enjoy today. The danger is to carry that shallowness into our relationship with God. Nathan addresses a theme that is so relevant for the church today: going deeper with God. He faces with honesty and personal experience the hindrances that stop believers doing just that. This book will prove to be an encouragement to all believers seeking a more impacting and effective relationship with God.

Brent Douglas, Senior Leader, Encounter Christian Centre, Auckland, New Zealand.

Nathan Shaw's text on passion and fire is a great challenge to all believers. It is a challenge to those who walk in the lowlands and the valleys of Christian living. It is a challenge to climb the mountain of God, to meet with God. The mountain is a place where there is no human fog or smog, where everything is clean, clear and the air is pure. Nathan's book is a call to the Bride of Christ to really and truly enter into intimacy with the Bridegroom, our Lord Jesus Christ. May God bless the text to all who read.

Kevin J Conner, Author, Melbourne, Australia.

Passion and Fire will encourage all those who yearn for greater intimacy with God, and particularly those who struggle to obtain it. I am glad that Nathan has shared some of his story and opened his life for those who want to learn from it. Daniel 11:32 says that those who truly know their God will be strong and do exploits. A lost world awaits such as these.

Dudley Hall, Author, Founder and President of Successful Christian Living Ministries, Contributing Editor of *The Morning Star Journal*. www.sclm.org

Nathan Shaw's *Passion and Fire* fulfills its title. I was moved, stirred, challenged and filled with a sense of the awe of God as I read through its pages. Nathan's clarion call for individuals to see the presence of God more than the gifts of God insures the gifts will always be present for those who are humble, hungry and thirsty. You should be prepared to be changed as you read through his book *Passion and Fire*.

John Paul Jackson, Author, Founder of Streams Ministries International. www.streamsministries.com

Nathan Shaw has opened our eyes to a realm of God's presence and intimate relationship with Christ Jesus. Thanks Nathan for sharing your personal experiences and challenging us to fulfill Father God's heart by coming into a personal, committed relationship with Jesus Christ. The reading of this book should renew a passion for Jesus Christ and inflame the reader with the fire of the Holy Spirit.

Dr. Bill Hamon, Author, Chairman and Founder of Christian International Ministries Network, President of Christian International Business Network.

God is calling us to be His friend. He is looking for men and women through whom His purposes in the earth can be birthed. Nathan's book *Passion and Fire* will kindle the passion in you to be one in whom God can share His intimate secrets. Reading this book will cause a passion for intimacy to rise in you that will affect a hurting world.

Bob Mumford, Author.

Passion and fire is exactly what this challenging book is all about. Nathan Shaw bares his heart's longing to see the church brought into a deeper intimacy with Christ. Unlike many who swing the pendulum for intimacy into a mystical and monastical extreme, Shaw brings a healthy balance with his emphasis on reaching the lost. May God use this book as a spiritual accelerant to ignite a fresh burden for intimacy and involvement. I commend it to you.

David Ravenhill, Author.

I read Nathan Shaw's *Passion and Fire* with great interest. The book is about experiencing God, and Nathan explores this theme through many people throughout Scripture. He includes something of his own struggles to reach that intimacy. Some of these passages were to me redolent of the writings of some of my earlier godly models. But those men were all older, more mature. This is a book by a young man, eager to share with freshness and vitality the experience of closeness with God which he has come to have. The book, however, is not limited to any personal mystic experience. The last chapters of the book turn this intimacy into passion for Christ's last Great Commission to make disciples.

Rev Dr. David Stewart, Principal of The Bible College of New Zealand, 1965-1988.

Nathan asks the powerful question, 'Where Are The People of Passion?' I want to raise my hand in answer to that question and say, 'Here I am.' But is that an honest response or a desired one? This book makes clear the process of becoming a passionate and powerful person who knows his or her God intimately.

Iverna Tompkins. Author.

Passion and Fire is about pursuing intimacy with God. A young man's desire and passion for intimacy with his Creator has been combined with truth from others to produce a work from which we can all learn and build. Nathan has a way of allowing the reality of his personal relationship with God to overflow and impact his readers. His heart to help others understand some of the key principles of knowing God for who He truly is will motivate and inspire you to press further into your own pursuit of God. The combination of an all-powerful God and a man who knows the power of his God are evident all through the pages of this book.

Trevor Yaxley, Author, Co-Founder of Lifeway Ministries, Auckland, New Zealand. www.lifeway.ac.nz

FOREWORD BY JOHN SANDFORD

Passion and Fire is another book that the Lord is using to draw us into intimacy with Him. I have edited several books on this subject and written endorsements for more but, by far, this is the one I enjoyed the most.

All of these recent books call us to chase after God more fervently than ever before. This is the Holy Spirit's clarion call, sounding throughout the Church at this time. Nathan Shaw lifts that call beyond personal quests into God's greater purposes – for the work of ministry, for ushering in God's Kingdom on earth.

Nathan, like his namesake in the Old Testament, gently exposes the reasons for our resistance to intimacy, and tells us how to overcome them. He lifts away shame and guilt, not by exhausting lists of 'how to's' and 'how not to's', but by taking us into the loving arms of the Father. He reveals the Father's loving nature so that shame falls away like heavy frost melting off our stony hearts.

Other books in this field have left me feeling like I ought to try to find greater intimacy with God but not sure that I really wanted to. Perhaps it was just me, I don't mean it critically of others. But *Passion and Fire* rekindled desire within me. It was as if that desire had somehow become banked, requiring bellows to pump it into flame again – and again and again. The strain that I once felt to keep the fire aglow is gone. I just know that the fire is there, resident and alive, and God will fan my sparks to bonfires whenever His purposes prompt. I look forward not to laborious questing, but to restful flaming.

I believe this book will do the same for others. *Passion and Fire* puts the emphasis on God's desire to enter into relationship with us. The book also calls us to enter into more disciplined seeking. But Nathan makes the case for God's grace so strongly that the onus of labor is lifted off us, and discipline and seeking become joyful and easy responses rather than stressful work.

A sense of joy undergirds the book. Not ecstatic peaks that pass and plunge into melancholy and despair, but a quiet river that you can step into at any time. This book leaves me resting in the biblical knowledge that the river is a bubbling stream that lives within me. I don't have to refind it, I only need to rest in it and experience it.

In the end, it is simply all about God. God is the first Chaser, not us. The spring of joy bubbles up from that fact. For, 'Herein is love, not that we first loved God, but that He first loved us.'

CONTENTS

Prologue	15
Part 1: A Dynamic Encounter	21
1. Face to Face	23
Part 2: A Legacy of Passion	31
2. The Call, the Promise and the Covenant	33
3. Consuming Fire	45
4. The Baptism of Fire	51
Part 3: Obstacles that Keep Us from the Secret Place	65
5. The Secret Place	67
6. The Great Deception	81
7. Drawing Near to God	95
8. The Enclosed Garden: A Story	101
Part 4: The Outward Mission	109
9. The Father's Desire	111
10. Intercepting Our Generation	123
11. Igniting Passion for the Lost	135
Part 5: Entering God's Embrace	147
12. The Story of God and Mankind	149
Epilogue	161

PROLOGUE

There is a fresh wind blowing across the Body of Christ. Wherever this wind blows it awakens fiery passion for our heavenly Bridegroom, Jesus. We were created for divine romance, and many are beginning to discover the beauty of that romance.

Much of the theme of *Passion and Fire* centers around the relationship the Church has with Jesus as our heavenly Bridegroom. John the Baptist, Jesus, Paul and John all refer to this relationship between Christ and His Church using the term 'Bridegroom' for Jesus and 'Bride' for the Church. The Bride of Christ is made up of men and women. Men often find it hard to embrace this concept. It may be helpful to understand that John the Baptist, Jesus, Paul and John all embodied the true masculine spirit. It would be hard to find men who were more 'manly' than these four. They use the terminology 'Bridegroom' and 'Bride' because it best describes the depth, focus and unity of love we can have with Christ. By being part of Christ's Bride, men in no way diminish their masculinity; in fact they enhance it. If this concept is still hard to embrace consider that both men and women are referred to as 'Sons of God' throughout the New Testament. By being 'Sons of God' women in no way diminish their femininity; to the contrary they enhance it. We are called to be both 'Sons of God' and 'The Bride of Christ'.

God is not looking for a corporate institution to carry out His will on the earth. Rather, He is longing for a body made up of those who have determined to give themselves to Him with undivided devotion. God is looking for a Bride not an institution. The difference is this: the corporate institution does what it thinks God wants and assumes or hopes that He will approve. The Bride of Christ, on the other hand, is less concerned with 'moving mountains' in His name and more concerned with moving His heart. Tragically most of the Christian world fails to move the heart of God. Without His help we are doomed to the slog and sweat that our own human effort produces. He longs for us to abandon our futile striving and simply let Him love us. We cannot move the heart of God until we are first moved by His love for us (1 John 4:19). It is time to cease our frantic service and discover the joy of sacrificial love.

I have written this book with two groups in mind – those who have experienced and embraced this fresh wind and those who, for whatever reason, have not. I have become increasingly burdened for people who yearn to know true passion for God but are continually defeated in their pursuit of Him. Whether you struggle to experience and know intimacy with God or not, I invite you to come on a journey that will take us deeper into the heart of God. The following story illustrates the path we must tread.

The Mountain Village – A Story

The mountain village was full of activity, with people rushing to and fro, intent on meeting the agendas and deadlines of the many and various projects in which they were engaged. New buildings could be seen throughout the village and many more were in construction, each edifice bigger and better than the one before. There were conference centers, meeting halls and places for recreation, prayer, counseling, publishing and recording.

This was my town, the place I had grown up. I had my first encounter with Jesus here. The years had been filled with rich experiences, encountering and discovering God. But recently I had been gripped with an unrelenting dis-ease and dissatisfaction. The things that once delighted and satisfied me now seemed lifeless and empty. In vain I tried to find the fullness I had previously experienced, throwing myself into activities that had once brought satisfaction and life. But no matter how hard I tried, it felt like I was getting drawn further away from the God I loved. In desperation I cried out to Him.

'God, why does my heart seem so cold and isolated from you? Awaken my heart to fervency and passion. Draw me close to You again!' Even my desperate cry sounded hollow and empty.

I continued to work in the village and do what I had always done – meeting, sharing, praying, building, listening, serving and caring. Some people noticed the change in me and tried to make me rejoice and be happy. But all I could do was put on a mask, pretending to be something I wasn't. I knew God hated hypocrisy and I loved truth too much to live a lie.

'God, what are you doing?'

I felt so distant from the Lord. But I continued to seek Him and began to look for and notice Him in places I hadn't before. One of those places was the mountains. The mountains that towered above our village were majestic, and it wasn't that I hadn't noticed them before, it's just that now they seemed to speak and beckon in a new way. Looking up the slopes, I could hear the voice of God calling me to come away and be with Him.

This was no small thing. I knew that if I went up into the mountains, I would have to leave everything that had been familiar to me. God was calling me to get lost in His immensity as the One who has no beginning and no end. I began to see a side of Him that is awesome, holy and majestic, but also frightening. I was starting to recognise the 'goodness and severity of God' (Romans 11:22). Everything in my flesh resisted knowing One who was so profoundly holy, but the yearning in my spirit would not be satisfied until I did. Below me in the village was a life that was mundane and predictable; above me in the mountains was a life of wild adventure that would demand levels of courage and trust beyond anything I had ever known. I had to take the risk. I couldn't bear to live as I was for a moment longer, and as the mountains continued to speak, I knew I had to respond.

'Lord give me strength to scale the heights. Let Your perfect love cast out the fear of coming to know You as You truly are.'

Then I heard the Lord's voice speak into my heart, 'I will make your feet like the feet of a deer, I will enable you to go on the heights.'

My heart eagerly responded, 'Sovereign Lord, *You* are my strength, *make* my feet like the feet of a deer, *enable* me to go on the heights.'

This is what I was created for! That night I slept with anticipation in my heart. The next day I would start the ascent.

As word spread about my ventures into the mountains, some people were uneasy. They preferred things to be safer and more predictable. I was part of the village and always would be – but now I was learning to be part of the mountains. Each day I would climb higher as the Lord made my feet stronger and more secure on the rugged heights. The higher I went the clearer the air became. My perceptions became sharper as I began to see as He sees. As I climbed further, I was captured not only with breath-taking views but also the tender, intimate surprises of God. I never knew when I would stumble across a beautiful mountain flower in stark contrast to the barren, rugged terrain. As I became more and more part of the mountains, the changes were reflected in my heart. The mountains were timeless. They kissed eternity. I was reminded of what Jesus said, 'This is eternal life: that they may know You, the only true God, and Jesus Christ whom You have sent' (John 17:3). Jesus and the Father became the very air I breathed.

One day I came to the top of the mountains. Far below, I could see the village – the people I knew and loved. I felt God's heart for them in a way I'd never experienced. Some of them had begun to ask me about the mountains and I knew God was stirring them as He had me. Looking up into the heavens I felt God's love envelope me as He opened my eyes to see into His heart. I could see Jesus praying to the Father the words of Paul in Ephesians 3, 'Father let them know how wide and long and high and deep is My love. Let them know this love that surpasses knowledge.' My heart began to break as He enlarged it to feel some of what He feels. This was a call to make His intercession my own. As I looked out over the mountains, I could see the nations torn apart by hatred and strife, controlled by false religion and deception. War, famine and disease engulfed entire nations, while materialism, greed and pleasure engulfed others. It was more than I could bear.

'Lord, have mercy! Release Your end-time harvesters into the nations of the earth.'

As I looked down into the valley I could see the village. The sun was still shining and it looked peaceful and serene. But above the mountains, storm clouds were gathering. I knew that when the storm came many in the village would be devastated – some would even become angry and turn away from God. But the only place of safety was in His embrace.

'Lord, awaken the people of the village. Let them not be deceived and blinded about the approaching storms. Call them to come up the mountain and meet with You face to face. Give courage and strength to those who respond. Let them be able to say, "The Sovereign Lord is my strength. He makes my feet like the feet of a deer, He enables me to go on the heights."'

Do you long to go up onto the heights and be face to face with Jesus?

All journeys have a starting place, and even after experiencing the fresh wind of intimacy with God over the last fifteen years, I continually find myself back at the beginning, learning lessons in a new way. Relationships are cultivated and this is certainly no less true when it comes to our relationship with God. The principles of cultivation are simple, but there are no short cuts. In this book we will examine the spiritual legacy of passion left by those who have gone before us; the starting place for holy passion and some of the roadblocks that keep us from it; the outward mission of passion; and the culmination of holy passion between Christ and His Bride.

But what does passion and fire look like? Over the years, I have made a number of missionary trips to the South Pacific nation of Vanuatu. One trip in particular stands out from the rest. I found myself in the middle of an intense outpouring of God's Spirit. The level of passion and devotion I witnessed and experienced during this time was life changing. Let me tell you the story.

Part 1:

A DYNAMIC ENCOUNTER

FACE TO FACE

I boarded the plane and found my seat. After carefully placing my rather heavy hand-luggage under the seat in front of me, I sat down. I didn't want to put it in the overhead locker because I didn't think it would fit. As usual, I found the two ends of my seatbelt, fastened them and pulled the extension until it fitted comfortably. Now apart from reading the emergency procedure card, which I fairly well knew by heart, all I could do was wait. I loved flying, but after so many flights it had lost its initial appeal. This was my third missionary trip to Vanuatu, a small nation of 83 islands in the South Pacific. To get to my destination in the north of Vanuatu, I still had a handful of flights to board and disembark. I was unsure what the next two months would hold. Despite having gone through one of the most difficult periods of my life, I had set my heart on going to Vanuatu again.

As the hostess read through the emergency procedures, my mind went back three years to the time when God first moved my heart to go to Vanuatu. My Uncle and Aunty, Walter and Faith Molloy, had taught in a school in Vanuatu for a couple of years. After this they had gone back as missionaries on short mission trips. It was one of their letters home that captured me. In it they described their involvement in a powerful deliverance session in which the person they were praying for was dramatically set free from the powers of darkness. The power and reality of demonic activity in nations like Vanuatu is something that goes way beyond the comprehension of most western minds. This deliverance session had been an intense battle, a life and death struggle – not just a casual casting off of some evil spirits. After reading the letter, my heart was gripped and I couldn't sleep that night.

Not long after this, Walter and Faith came to my town as part of a Team Missions group. For a month, six revival meetings were held per week and the presence and power of God during this time was amazing. Nobody wanted to miss a single meeting. In the midst of this, I spoke to Walter and Faith about my desire to go with them on their next trip to Vanuatu. They were keen for me to come but gave me a number of conditions – I had to improve my physical fitness, learn to play the guitar, get ministry experience at church and change my raw energy diet. So I diligently set about teaching myself the guitar and doing aerobics. Within eight months the time had come.

It wasn't easy leaving home for the first time. In Vanuatu, the culture shock took its toll. I was living in remote villages with no electricity or running water, a bucket of cold water for a shower, a hole in the ground for a toilet, a grass hut for shelter, and food that I had to acquire a taste for. But I loved working with my uncle and aunty during the six weeks I was with them. Walter became like a father to me, and it was a great joy for him to watch me respond to an unfamiliar environment. I was captured by his heart for the people of Vanuatu. Sometimes, when he thought about them, tears would come to his eyes. He was motivated not merely by human love but a deep compassion that came from the heart of God. Walter and Faith recognized the call of God on my life and gave me the opportunity to develop in it. I loved them for this. After returning home I was eager to return the next year.

Little did I know how emotionally shattering the following year would be. One week into my second visit, Walter and Faith returned to New Zealand. Walter was unwell and I was left to continue the trip alone. I was 21, working solo in a foreign culture and ministering in villages where the spiritual atmosphere was hard and uninviting. It was the most difficult experience of my life, but somehow I managed to survive. After about four weeks, I developed a nasty boil on my knee. The pain was excruciating and I had to put up with it for another week or two before I returned home exhausted and drained.

In the aftermath of this trip I experienced three major losses one after the other. The sickness that forced Walter to return to New Zealand turned out to be cancer in his liver. It was fatal, and within a few months he died. Just after this my pastor was moved to another church. He, like Walter, had seen the call of God on my life and had allowed me to take the Wednesday night Holy Spirit meetings we were holding at church. Through these meetings people had been revived, refreshed, strengthened and empowered. I was free to move in the Spirit without limitations, and God had met us in powerful ways. I had come to know and love the Holy Spirit as a person of great depth and creativity, and by far the greatest loss for me was the loss of His manifest presence. The Holy Spirit had become more real to me than anyone else, He was everything I lived for and had built my life around – but now it felt like He was distant.

It was six months later and I was returning to Vanuatu for the third time. The sound of the plane engines powering up for take off interrupted my thoughts. We started to hurtle down the runway. As the speed of the plane caused me to be pushed backwards into my seat, I couldn't help but wonder what was ahead. The plane lifted off the runway and I was on my way – little did I realize what God was about to do.

It was good to be back in Vanuatu. I love the warm tropical weather, particularly after leaving the cold winter of the South Island of New Zealand. I was staying with Pastor Raynold Bori and his wife Joy. Raynold is the director of Every Home for Christ Vanuatu and was the person organizing my itinerary for the next two months. During the first two weeks, I only preached a few times, spending most days having a holiday. I found this a little frustrating particularly as the plans kept changing. More than once it was organized for me to speak, only for the arrangements to be cancelled. Despite this, the Holy Spirit moved powerfully at the few meetings I was involved with. It felt as if something new was happening, like God had an appointment with these people.

After one meeting, the worshippers were so overcome with God's anointing that they had to be carried out of the building so it could be locked for the night. Undoubtedly the most significant meeting was when I spoke on Spirit-empowered prayer. After I spoke I selected seven people and asked them to come to the front. I wanted to use them as an illustration of how we can open up to the Holy Spirit during prayer meetings.

I got them to face toward the congregation, take a step forward, lift their hands and say, 'Come Holy Spirit, consume me.' No sooner said than done, the Holy Spirit began to touch them powerfully. After a short time I asked them to open their eyes and be like they were before they lifted their hands. I was wanting to demonstrate that we can open up to God in everyday life and have Him touch us. I got them to repeat the procedure, walking through it with them.

Take a step forward.

Lift your hands.

Say 'Come Holy Spirit consume me.'

This time the Holy Spirit gripped them with intercession and they ended up on the floor weeping. One of the seven was Raynold's wife, Joy. She testified that while God was touching her, she felt great love for the lost and didn't want any of them to miss eternal life. Naturally, I was delighted to have my message backed up with such a dynamic illustration! I was pleased with the meeting but had no idea of the impact it would ultimately have.

Joy led the children's ministry, and the children would often come to Raynold and Joy's house to practise and perfect dances that they had made up to Christian music. These nine to thirteen-year-old children shared the same evangelistic fervor as the Every Home for Christ ministry. They had been practicing for an upcoming trip to Vanuatu's capital, Port Vila. During the week-long trip there would be evangelistic meetings held every night. Port Vila is a one and a half hour flight on a 20-seat Twin Otter plane, and for many of the children it would be their first time away from their own island of Santo. Being the capital, Port Vila is the nation's link with the rest of the world, making it much more commercial and westernized. Six weeks prior to the trip, the children fasted every day until 5 p.m. They had found this difficult for the first week, but after this they were fine and, from what I could see, didn't seem to lack energy.

The day after the meeting where I spoke on Spirit-empowered prayer, the children spent much of the morning practicing their dances. Once they had finished Joy led them in a time of prayer. Having been dramatically touched herself the night before, she was encouraging them to open up to the Holy Spirit. For the next hour and a half they laughed, wept and shook as God touched them powerfully. I watched in awe at the hunger and desperation they had for God. During this time many of them began to have visions. Three of them saw Jesus.

Nothing could stop these children. Every time they would meet, they were eager to wait on the Holy Spirit and let Him touch them. One night as this was happening, one of the girls, called Pauline, had a vision. In the vision she saw a dove with an olive branch in its mouth. The dove whispered to her, 'The fire is in the middle (of the room), everyone has to go to the middle because the fire will burn out your sins.' Pauline told this to the rest of the children and they all went to the middle of the room. The fire of God came on them in such intensity they started vigorously rubbing their arms, legs, faces and bodies because of the heat they could feel. I had never seen anything like this before. It was like their bodies were literally on fire. These children were obviously experiencing something similar to what the prophet Isaiah experienced when a live coal of fire touched his lips (Isaiah 6:1-8).

Hebrews 12:29 says, 'Our God is a consuming fire.' The Greek word used here for 'consume' means to consume *utterly*. It does not speak of a small tameable fire but rather a consuming, intense fire. As the children continued to meet over the next few weeks the same intensity of God's fire manifested itself again and again.

In Vanuatu plans often change. You learn quickly that nothing is quite as certain or definite as it is made out to be. Ni-Vanuatu (the people of Vanuatu) call this 'coconut time'. You don't know when a coconut is going to fall off a tree – things just happen when they happen. It's part of the relaxed, laid back way people live in the islands. As usual my itinerary changed, and I ended up with an extra flight coupon. Raynold asked me if I would use it to fly to Vila for the week with the children's ministry and be part of the crusade there. I was offered two to three hours each morning to hold revival meetings. So, after some deliberation, I decided to go.

The children had put hours of work into practicing their dances. Costumes had been made and many other things had to be organized (someone donated a cow which had to be chopped up and taken with us). We took the one and a half hour flight to Vila in two lots because we couldn't all fit into the aeroplane. In Vila, a dormitory had been hired from a government department for our accommodation.

For the first two days we used the adjacent dining room to hold our morning revival meetings. No local people came (it was too far away and people work during the day in Vila), so it was just those staying in the dormitory (Raynold and Joy, the children, a group of intercessors, children's workers and organizational workers). The children had experienced so much of God I was keen to give them some teaching and focus in the midst of it all. What I had to say was short and simple. I had to teach them to be considerate of other people because often they would get drunk in the spirit and not think of those around them. I didn't want anyone getting hurt. After the first day Raynold came to me and said he wanted us to hold the meetings much earlier so we wouldn't disturb the people who worked at the facility. The next day he decided we should use the hallway in the dormitory for our meeting. I can't say I was too impressed. The planned revival meetings which were supposed to span the morning and have local attendance now started at five in the morning, were in a dormitory hallway and were mostly a bunch of kids with a few adults. There was no doubt about their hunger for God, but it certainly wasn't what I had agreed to come to Vila to do.

The crusade meetings at night were citywide. They had an attendance of about a thousand and went for hours. True to Vanuatu style every church group would do an item. The children's dances were definitely the most popular and the most anointed. Raynold would preach and God was moving powerfully. We would get back to the dormitory after midnight, have a drink and go to bed at about 1 a.m. Getting up at 5 a.m. meant only four hours sleep. I tried to tell Raynold that children (and adults) need more sleep than this, particularly when doing crusade meetings every night. Needless to say, such wisdom was ignored. They were having revival and nothing was going to stop them. God was moving, the hunger level was high and no sacrifice was considered too great.

It was Friday morning – I could hear the sound of the children talking and interacting as I stirred from my few hours of sleep. Opening my eyes to locate my watch I reached over to check the time. Five o'clock. After lying still for a short while I dragged myself out of bed and got ready to face the day. When I appeared, the children were already waiting, sitting leaning against the two walls on either side of the hallway. I spoke from Isaiah 6 about the importance of seeking God's face and not just His hand. Seeking God's face speaks of relationship and intimacy, whereas seeking His hand speaks of looking for what God can do for you. After speaking, I laid hands on them and the Holy Spirit's presence was tangible. There was a sense of holiness about what God was doing. This went on for a period of time and then it happened…

Suddenly, unexpectedly, the face of Jesus appeared on the concrete wall at the end of the dormitory. Some of the children were the first to notice. They gasped in surprise, pointing at the wall on which the face had appeared. The rest of us were instantly drawn by their exclamations and pointing fingers. In stunned awe we quickly moved toward the face. I will never forget the things that happened over the next hour and a half. We were so caught up in pouring out love and affection toward Jesus, that any onlooker would have been frightened at our level of passion as we wept, cried out, and kissed and hugged the wall.

During the ministry time I did not realize that Raynold had left. He had gone to collect a small bus which he had hired to take us all on a scenic tour of Port Vila and the surrounding district. When he returned from collecting the bus he approached the entrance to the dormitory and was overwhelmed with the power and depth of God's presence. He broke down weeping and told me afterwards that the whole hallway was permeated with a cloud.

I found out later, that when the intercessors had been praying the night before, they had prophetically seen the face of Jesus appearing on the wall. Also Humphries (one of the children) saw Jesus in the meeting the night before. Jesus told him that He would meet with him in his bedroom the next day. He most certainly did!

I think we would have happily stayed before the Lord all day except that the bus Raynold hired had to be returned at a certain time. We reluctantly went. It took us a while to settle after the impact of our encounter with God, and as soon as the tour was over, we rushed back to the dormitory to find the face still on the wall. The presence of God surrounded the whole dormitory and we spent two days in awe of Him. When we left later the next day, the face was still there. We could come and meet with Him anytime. There was always a group of people at the end of the hallway, worshipping, dancing, standing in awe or simply prostrate. God did a deep work in our lives.

Why does God do things like this? If we could always explain God, He wouldn't be God. The Bible tells us about signs and wonders. A sign points to something of significance. Its purpose is to make the thing it points to known. A wonder is something that causes you to marvel and stand in awe. The Greek word also carries with it the implication of something with prophetic significance. I believe God is raising up a generation who will live with the sole ambition of being 'in His face'. 'For it is the God who commanded light to shine out of darkness who has shone in our hearts to give the light of the knowledge of the glory of God in the face of Jesus Christ' (2 Corinthians 4:6).

The cry of this generation will be that of the shulamite woman in Song of Solomon 1:2, 'Let him kiss me with the kisses of his mouth – for your love is better than wine.' This expresses a longing to know the Lord experientially. Many acknowledge God's love but only a few go on to pursue a relationship of intimacy and depth. To desire the kisses of His mouth requires being prepared to literally be 'in His face'. It also means being prepared to let Him be in our faces.

The whole book of Revelation testifies about a people who are 'in His face' (for example Revelation 5:11-14). When John saw Jesus in Revelation chapter 1, he fell down like a dead man. John had already fallen prostrate before Jesus when He saw him transfigured (Matthew 17). Now Jesus, having died and been resurrected, appeared fully glorified. Humans cannot handle this much glory. In Vanuatu we saw a faint image on a wall as a prophetic sign. What will happen when multitudes from every nation live in hot pursuit of the full glory of Jesus' face?

Part 2:

A LEGACY OF PASSION

THE CALL, THE PROMISE & THE COVENANT

Days of Fire

Even a cursory overview of the Scriptures reveals that the 'last days' – the time between Christ's ascension and return – will be days of great intensity, great conflict and fire. We face increasing darkness *and* increasing light. 'Arise, shine; for your light has come! And the glory of the Lord is risen upon you. For behold, the darkness shall cover the earth, and deep darkness the people; but the Lord will arise over you, and His glory will be seen upon you' (Isaiah 60:1-2). From the book of Malachi we learn two things about the 'days of fire':

1. As the fire of God's presence increases, anything that is combustible is consumed (Malachi 3:1-5).

2. The fire of God is manifested primarily through people who have come to know Him as a consuming fire (Malachi 4:1-3).

From the time Adam and Eve were created God has passionately pursued intimate relationship with mankind. Throughout history people have known God in different ways – Saviour, Deliverer, Protector, Provider, Comforter etc. Few, however, have gone on to know Him as a consuming fire, although He makes this invitation to every one of us. To know God as a consuming fire is to enter into a depth of relationship that supersedes all human comprehension or understanding.

We have been given a profound spiritual legacy from the passionate seekers of God throughout history. Our failure to realize this legacy results in a Christianity that is often shallow and passionless. Without understanding our spiritual foundations we are utterly powerless to face these last days. If we neglect the spiritual foundations laid by those who have gone before us we become subject to mediocrity and a religion that is mainly about comfort and ease. We cannot enter into a glorious future unless we understand these foundations. Consider the example of Enoch.

Enoch

Scripture records that Enoch, the seventh descendent of Adam, walked with God (Genesis 5:24). After walking with God for 300 years he had developed such a close relationship to God that he simply took one more step and ended up in God's realm. Enoch never died.

Before Adam and Eve sinned, they would walk in the garden with God. Adam was still alive when Enoch was young, so it is likely that Enoch would have heard from him first hand what it was like to walk with God. A desire for that must have burned in his heart.

Enoch simply refused to live without knowing the full glory of an intimate relationship with God. He was a man of perseverance and courage and an example to all of us. Enoch didn't stop until he was completely enveloped by God's embrace. He got there by taking one step at a time. God loves that attitude. Three hundred years is a long time to press into God. We can so easily give up after only five minutes or five days.

Not much is known about Enoch's life. But the life of Abram gives us a much fuller understanding of the details of what it means to walk with God.

The God Encounter

When God wants to accomplish something on earth, He first looks for a man or woman through whom His purposes can be fulfilled. Abram was such a man. It took only one encounter with God to completely change the direction of his life. 'The God of glory appeared to our father Abraham when he was in Mesopotamia, before he dwelt in Haran, and said to him, "Get out of your country and from your relatives, and come to a land that I will show you"' (Acts 7:2-3).

After God appeared to him, Abram was no longer able to continue on with life as normal. Hebrews 11:8-10 says, 'By faith Abraham obeyed when he was called to go out to the place which he would receive as an inheritance. And he went out, not knowing where he was going. By faith he dwelt in the land of promise as in a foreign country, dwelling in tents with Isaac and Jacob, the heirs with him of the same promise; for he waited for the city which has foundations, whose builder and maker is God.'

Abram's encounter with God resulted in him reaching out for all that God had in store. His eyes had been opened on a heavenly and spiritual level. In the material world, Abram had wealth and prestige. Now God was calling him to pursue a heavenly city infinitely superior to anything on earth (Hebrews 11:13-16). Abram left behind what was familiar to him and became a stranger and a pilgrim in a foreign land. To know God as a consuming fire, we will need to follow Abram's example.

Abram's pursuit of God began with an encounter with God. But this was just the first of a number of such encounters throughout his life.

Desperate for God

After God reveals Himself to us in a new dimension, He waits for us to respond to Him and pursue Him with greater tenacity. After Abram left his own country and journeyed to Canaan, the Bible says that he 'passed through the land to the place of Shechem, as far as the terebinth tree of Moreh. And the Canaanites were then in the land. Then the Lord appeared to Abram and said, "To your descendants I will give this land." And there he built an altar to the Lord, who had appeared to him. And he moved from there to the mountain east of Bethel, and he pitched his tent with Bethel on the west and Ai on the east; there he built an altar to the Lord and called on the name of the Lord' (Genesis 12:6-8).

As soon as God appeared to him, Abram built an altar as an act of worship and consecration. It wasn't, however, until he was away from the Canaanite settlements that he called on the name of the Lord. It is not unusual for God to encounter us in a public setting but it is usually in private that the true wrestling for intimacy with God begins. After responding to His initial encounters and forsaking everything else in pursuit of Him, we are left with nothing else to fall back on but Him. As a foreigner in a foreign land, Abram had nothing but God. God weans us away from our former dependencies, and asks again and again, 'How hungry are you for Me?'

Where are the desperate hearts that will not be satisfied until fiery passion for God has consumed every atom and fiber of their beings? Where are those who cry out day and night for the living God, desperate to appear before Him who alone can satisfy the cravings of the human heart (Psalm 42:1-3)? Thirst is one of the most intense cravings known to man. God calls us to have this kind of desperation for Him, the fountain of all life.

God was bringing Abram to the place where He could reveal Himself as the God of consuming fire.

A Fiery Encounter

After these things the word of the Lord came to Abram in a vision, saying, 'Do not be afraid, Abram. I am your shield, your exceedingly great reward.'

But Abram said, 'Lord God, what will You give me, seeing I go childless, and the heir of my house is Eliezer of Damascus?' Then Abram said, 'Look, You have given me no offspring; indeed one born in my house is my heir!' And behold, the word of the Lord came to him, saying, 'This one shall not be your heir, but one who will come from your own body shall be your heir.' Then He brought him outside and said, 'Look now toward heaven, and count the stars if you are able to number them.' And He said to him, 'So shall your descendants be.' And he believed in the Lord, and He accounted it to him for righteousness. Then He said to him, 'I am the Lord, who brought you out of Ur of the Chaldeans, to give you this land to inherit it.' And he said, 'Lord God, how shall I know that I will inherit it?' So He said to him, 'Bring Me a three-year-old heifer, a three-year-old female goat, a three-year-old ram, a turtledove,

The Call, the Promise and the Covenant

and a young pigeon.' Then he brought all these to Him and cut them in two, down the middle, and placed each piece opposite the other; but he did not cut the birds in two. And when the vultures came down on the carcasses, Abram drove them away. Now when the sun was going down, a deep sleep fell upon Abram; and behold, horror and great darkness fell upon him. Then He said to Abram: 'Know certainly that your descendants will be strangers in a land that is not theirs, and will serve them, and they will afflict them four hundred years. And also the nation whom they serve I will judge; afterward they shall come out with great possessions. Now as for you, you shall go to your fathers in peace; you shall be buried at a good old age. But in the fourth generation they shall return here, for the iniquity of the Amorites is not yet complete.' And it came to pass, when the sun went down and it was dark, that behold, there appeared a smoking oven and a burning torch that passed between those pieces. On the same day the Lord made a covenant with Abram, saying: 'To your descendants I have given this land, from the river of Egypt to the great river, the River Euphrates' (Genesis 15:1-18).

When Abram left Ur of the Chaldeans, the only assurance he had was a promise from God. Undoubtedly this took great faith. The above encounter happened after Abram had been living in Canaan for a number of years. Earlier, in Genesis 13, God had reaffirmed to Abram the promise of inheriting the land. Abram was to get up and walk through the length and width of the land to see what had been promised. But Abram still had no understanding of how he would inherit the land, particularly as his wife was barren and they had no children. When God said to Abram in Genesis 15:1, 'I am your shield, your exceedingly great reward', it was true Abram had nothing else but God. Abram enquired, 'Lord God, how shall I know that I will inherit it?' In response to this question God confirmed His promise by entering into a covenant with Abram.

A covenant is the most serious, solemn agreement that any person can make. It is an act of supreme allegiance to another person. Such an agreement is so serious that to break it is to invite serious consequences on one's life. Our God is a God of covenant. Not only does He enter into a covenant with us but He also invites us to enter into a covenant with Him. In a covenant relationship everything that belongs to one person also becomes the other's. If an enemy attacks a person who is in a covenant, the covenantal partner will treat that enemy as his or her own.

A covenant was always formed by the shedding of blood, symbolic of laying down your life for another. The two parties would walk between the two halves of the sacrificial animals. In this particular covenant only God came down and walked between the pieces. Because this was a one-sided covenant, there was nothing Abram could do that would cause the covenant to be broken. This was the highest assurance God could give to Abram. It was also a revelation to Abram of God's desire to enter into a covenant with mankind and an invitation for Abram to enter into a covenant with God.

The Bible says that a 'deep sleep' fell on Abram. This Hebrew word can also be translated 'a trance.' This was more than just a natural sleep, it was a profound and deep supernatural experience during which God revealed to Abram the future of the nation of Israel. Abram was allowed to experience the actual horror and darkness of suffering and affliction that the Israelites would go through. It was also a revelation of the heart of God concerning the Israelites' future suffering.

In 2 Chronicles 20:7 it says that Abraham was God's friend. There are very few people that the Bible records as God's friends. To be God's friend is a high distinction. 'Friends', in this usage, are those who have entered into such a depth of trust and openness with each other that they are able to share the deepest secrets of their hearts. This is what God did with Abram on this occasion. After sharing His heart with Abram, God came down as a consuming fire and walked between the sacrificial animals. Presumably, as was the custom, the animals were completely consumed.

To know God in His fullness and as He really is, is to know Him as a consuming fire. This experience is reserved for those who are willing to enter into a full covenant relationship with Him. It is not possible to define such a relationship in human terms – it supersedes anything that can be understood by the human mind.

'The secret of the Lord is with those who fear Him, and He will show them His covenant' (Psalm 25:14).

God wants to show us His covenant. In Ephesians 5:32, Paul called the covenantal relationship between Christ and the Church a great mystery. Within every unmarried, single person there is a yearning to enter into the covenant of marriage. But this is only a shadow of the yearning God put in us to enter into a covenant relationship with Him. When God reveals Himself to us, this yearning is awakened until such intense fervency grips our spirits that we are unable to accept anything less than being completely His. If God has begun to awaken this desire in your heart, now is the time to pursue Him with all your heart. Run and don't stop running until the flames of His love consume you.

Law or Promise

God gave Abram a promise. But this promise had nothing to do with Abram's righteousness. He did nothing to earn the promise, he simply had to respond to it in faith. Put more simply, he had to trust God to fulfill the promise. Receiving a promise always involves faith, which involves risk, which involves vulnerability. There is a sense of risk involved in responding to God's promises with simple faith. Without vulnerability there is no way to enter into a covenant. It means giving up our control to put ourselves at the mercy of another. Our past experiences and betrayed trust hinder this surrender.

Trust forms a safe environment for people to risk themselves with others. Abusive or absentee relationships cause this trust to be shattered. But it is God's heart to restore us from the effects of past negative experiences. To do this He has to melt our 'hearts of stone' with His love. Hearts of stone are formed when we continually protect ourselves from being hurt by those who are closest to us. There is a protective shell around our hearts. God slowly begins to break down these defences with His love. Often that process exposes the hurt and anger that is bottled inside, causing it to erupt, but it also brings pain out into the open where we can surrender it to God and receive His healing.

God's love is unconditional. It is not dependent on anything we have or have not done. To fully receive His love, however, we have to give up our hearts of stone and, with His help, forgive those who have hurt, abandoned, abused and betrayed us. The Law says that if a person hurts someone, he or she deserves to be hurt back. The Promise of God causes us to give unconditional love and favor to all, and to relinquish any claim to retaliation or punishment. The Law says that a person has to earn his own righteousness by doing the right thing and living up to a set of rules and regulations. The Promise affirms that we are already accepted because we have His righteousness. God's law is perfect (Psalm 19:7). Please note that by referring to the Law I am referring to its misuse, which is commonly called legalism.

We prefer to live by the Law because it means we do not have to surrender 'control'. The law is clearly defined and does not involve risking ourselves with others. It says, 'If I live by a particular standard of rules I will get that particular outcome.' Responding to the Promise, on the other hand, requires us to trust in God's faithfulness to fulfill His word. The contrast between the Law and the Promise is the same conflict that exists between the Spirit and the flesh. To live in the flesh is to live by our own standards and rules – whether they be 'fundamentalist', 'evangelical', 'pentecostal' or 'charismatic' – and to expect the anticipated outcome as our reward. To live in the Spirit is to surrender our control over our own destiny and trust the outcome to God. Such trust is what enabled Abram to leave all that was *familiar* and journey to a land that was completely *unfamiliar* to him.

Responding to the Promise leads to a life of adventure, excitement, risk, vulnerability and ultimately fulfillment. Living by the Law leads to a life that is predictable, boring, restricted, isolated and unfulfilled. Because it is so predictable it gives the illusion of being 'safe'. Those who live by the Law are unprepared to step out of their comfort zones. The Law focuses mostly on what we *cannot* do. The Promise focuses on what we *can* do, giving us wings to soar towards the fulfillment of our God-given destiny. God gives rules and boundaries to protect and nurture life rather than to stifle it and shut it down. Those who live by the Law vehemently oppose those who live by the Spirit. To live by God's promises will invite persecution and will require us to step out of our comfort zones. The apparent protective safety of the Law is a deception and an illusion. As terrifying as it is to the tendencies of our flesh, the safest and most secure place we can ever be is in the bonds of covenantal relationship with a God who is a consuming fire.

The God of Abraham, Isaac and Jacob

Experiencing passion and fire is a journey that takes us step by step into the heart of God. He stretches and challenges us, but He never gives us more than we can handle. If God revealed Himself to us fully it would be more than we could bear, so He progressively draws us closer. What is normal for one person may be overwhelming for another. What is overwhelming for us may be normal for someone else. God takes each of us from where we are.

It was about ten years after Abram left Ur that God revealed Himself to Abram as a God of consuming fire and entered into covenant with Him. After this encounter, Abram went out and tried to fulfill God's promise himself by having a child by Sarah's maidservant, Hagar. Thirteen years later, God appeared to Abram again. In this encounter (recorded in Genesis 17) Abram entered fully into a covenant with God. Circumcision was instituted as the sign of this covenant. The covenant in Genesis 15 was one-sided, whereas the covenant in Genesis 17 was two-sided. As a result of this covenant, Abram's name was changed to Abraham. Abram means 'exalted father', whereas Abraham means 'father of many nations'. The change of name was a confirmation of God's covenant promise to Abraham. As I noted earlier, in a covenant relationship everything you have also becomes the other person's. Now Abram's life would be irrevocably identified with God. This was signified by the name change. Likewise, God's name became identified with Abraham's. Frequently throughout scripture God is known as 'the God of Abraham, Isaac and Jacob'.

Soon after Abraham entered into this covenant with God, his wife Sarah conceived and gave birth to Isaac, the child of the promise. After Isaac had grown to childhood or adolescence, God tested Abraham's faithfulness.

The Test

The biggest test that Abraham went through (or any loving father could go through) was when God asked him to offer up Isaac as a sacrifice (Genesis 22:1-18). God waited until Abraham was about to slay Isaac before He intervened and provided a ram in Isaac's place. Abraham had passed the test. When Abraham entered into his covenant with God, everything he had now belonged to God, including Isaac, the child of the promise and Abraham's only son. Abraham proved his love for God and loyalty to the covenant by being prepared to give Isaac back to God. 'The secret of the Lord is with those who fear Him, and He will show them His covenant' (Psalm 25:14).

The Fear of God is an intense reverence, respect, love and esteem for God. Because Abraham feared God, God showed him His covenant. All the resources in the Universe are included in the provisions of this covenant. Abraham trusted in God's promise, knowing that if necessary Isaac would be resurrected from the dead through God's infinite power. Abraham trusted God so much that he was able to give up the thing that was most precious to him.

Abraham was probably about 115 years old when God asked him to offer up Isaac. He was 75 years old when he left Ur of the Chaldeans in response to God's promise and command. After a number of years God entered into a covenant with Abram revealing Himself as a consuming fire. At 99 years of age Abram entered into a covenant with God and became Abraham. From that time forward he walked with God (Genesis 17:1). After about 15 years of walking with God, he was tested and asked to offer up his only son. Our God is a jealous God and will not allow anything to come between Him and us.

Step by step He progressively leads us to the place of ultimate surrender to Him and ultimate fulfillment in Him until we can say like the Shulamite bride in Song of Solomon:

> Set me as a seal upon your heart,
> As a seal upon your arm;
> For love is as strong as death,

Jealousy as cruel as the grave;
Its flames are flames of fire,
A most vehement flame (Song of Solomon 8:6).

CONSUMING FIRE

The message of faith has often been proclaimed as a means of obtaining material wealth and blessing. Far more than this, faith is what causes us to reach for an intimate relationship with a God who is a consuming fire. As we have seen, Abraham's journey of faith caused him to draw closer and closer to this fire until he was completely captured by God's covenantal embrace. Even though the journey of faith is the wildest adventure anybody could ever embark on, the true message of faith has been watered down and taken out of context. Now it is barely recognizable.

We are true children of Abraham inasmuch as we walk in the same footsteps that Abraham walked (Galatians 3:7-9). Abraham died at the age of 175, but the covenant God confirmed to him was also confirmed to Abraham's son, Isaac, and to Isaac's son, Jacob. Throughout Scripture God is referred to as the God of Abraham, the God of Isaac, and the God of Jacob.

As God had promised, Abraham's descendants formed a vast nation and were forced into slavery by Pharaoh, King of Egypt. The Israelites suffered for many years under this cruel oppression before God raised up Moses as their deliverer. Through a miraculous set of events, Moses grew up in Pharaoh's house as the adopted son of Pharaoh's daughter. When he was 40 years old he was found guilty of murdering an Egyptian, so he fled the country and lived as a shepherd in the remote Sinai wilderness.

The Burning Bush

After Moses spent forty years tending sheep, God appeared to him in a burning bush. Four times during this encounter God referred to Himself as the God of Abraham, the God of Isaac, and the God of Jacob (Exodus 3:6,15,16,4:5). The primary purpose of God's visitation was to confirm the covenant that had been made with Abraham and his descendants. Soon afterwards, God almost killed Moses for not circumcising his son (Exodus 4:24). Through this event Moses learnt that God is serious about covenant relationships.

There is a link between God appearing as a consuming fire and the covenant relationship that He formed and entered into. Both Genesis 15 and Exodus 3 record encounters with God that are beyond human comprehension. They were profound, deep and holy meetings. Moses was commanded to take off his shoes because he stood on holy ground, and he hid his face because he was afraid to look at God. Today God is once again bringing His people to such a place.

Why did God wait so long before appearing to Moses? Forty years in a wilderness tending sheep seems like a terrible waste of time to us. But God's timetable is always different to ours. He is not impetuous, impatient or ambitious, and it is impossible to manipulate Him. In preparing our hearts to draw closer to Him, He knows exactly what He wants and waits patiently until His work is accomplished. How long will it take? As long as it takes. There is no point trying to push God by telling Him to hurry up. Often we think we are waiting on God when in fact He is waiting on us. He is a lot more patient with us than we are with Him.

The wilderness is a place where our agendas and ambitions slowly but surely die. During this time, humility was being developed in Moses' life. God was bringing him to a place where he could respond to God. Moses had to turn aside to meet God at the burning bush. A self-assertive person would be less inclined to turn aside – such an action would be an annoying inconvenience. It was, after all, not uncommon for a bush to be on fire in the wilderness. Moses had lived in the palaces of Egypt – but he met God on the backside of a desert. This lesson would remain with Moses for the rest of his life.

Why did God appear in the midst of a scruffy bush? Surely he could find a more dramatic way to make an appearance. There is nothing fancy about a bush. It is common and ordinary. But it seems that God always uses common and ordinary things to reveal His glory.

God has chosen the foolish things of the world to put to shame the wise, and God has chosen the weak things of the world to put to shame the things which are mighty; and the base things of the world and the things which are despised God has chosen, and the things which are not, to bring to nothing the things that are, that no flesh should glory in His presence (1 Corinthians 1:27-29).

For it is the God who commanded light to shine out of darkness, who has shone in our hearts to give the light of the knowledge of the glory of God in the face of Jesus Christ. But we have this treasure in earthen vessels, that the excellence of the power may be of God and not of us (2 Corinthians 4:6-7).

Moses' egocentricity was not completely broken during his forty years in the desert. In fact in some ways it was intensified. It took the encounter with God at the burning bush to confront Moses' pride. The wilderness is a place of routine – the same thing every day. After forty years of this wilderness routine, God commanded Moses to go as His mouthpiece and lead the Israelites out of their bondage in Egypt. Moses responded by arguing that he was inadequate for such a task. This false humility showed that Moses' self-obsession was still very much alive. He continued arguing until the anger of the Lord was kindled against him. Moses had to learn to trust in God rather than hiding behind his own inadequacy. Although he had been a murderer, he had to overcome his past sense of failure and learn to take God at His word.

Moses learned that although God is a consuming fire, He desires to dwell in the midst of things that are plain and ordinary in the eyes of men. The fire of God exposes and consumes the sin nature that is so contrary to Him. God's intention is not to destroy us, but for us to enter into the mysteries of a divine romance. Perhaps it is this revelation that enabled Moses to continually step into the fire of God's presence in the years that followed. Responding to God's word requires us to continually overcome inadequacy and fear. But we must respond to God's invitation, all the time crying out for courage and strength to make the journey.

No Other Gods

God's invitation to Abraham was only the beginning of His intentions. Ultimately God wanted to make this invitation to a whole nation (Exodus 19). When God came down on Mt Sinai to reveal Himself to the Israelites the sight was so awesome that they were gripped with fear.

> Now all the people witnessed the thunderings, the lightning flashes, the sound of the trumpet, and the mountain smoking; and when the people saw it, they trembled and stood afar off. Then they said to Moses, 'You speak with us, and we will hear; but let not God speak with us, lest we die.' And Moses said to the people, 'Do not fear; for God has come to test you, and that His fear may be before you, so that you may not sin.' So the people stood afar off, but Moses drew near the thick darkness where God was (Exodus 20:18-21).

Because the Israelites were frightened of God, they decided to make a golden calf to worship instead. At least a golden calf is safe and predictable. One glimpse of God's manifested glory will send us running to things that are familiar and safe. It is easy to point at the Israelites' inability to endure God's voice, but what makes us so sure that we wouldn't have acted the same way? Concerning the Israelites' journey through the wilderness, Paul says in 1 Corinthians 10:11-12, 'Now all these things happened to them as examples, and they were written for our admonition, upon whom the ends of the ages have come. Therefore let him who thinks he stands take heed lest he fall.'

These things were written not to show us that we are different from the Israelites, but to show us how much we are like them. If we heard God speak to us as He did to the Israelites, I suspect we too would run for shelter. Even God's voice has fire in it. There is so much of eternity in God's voice that it short-circuits our temporal minds and causes our flesh to respond in terror. The incredible thing is that as vast and infinite as God is, He passionately desires for us to come to know Him through the sacred bonds of a covenant relationship.

The first of the Ten Commandments is, 'You shall have no other gods before me' (Exodus 20:3). Fire does not consume fire, it only consumes that which is unlike itself. God wants us to become like Him by drawing near to Him. He yearns for us to be completely His. The fire of His holy jealousy will consume every god, every idol in our hearts. Only then can we be completely His. Only then can we see Him as He is and enter into the mysteries of His love.

Approaching God

Only Moses drew near the thick darkness where God was. Thick darkness represents the untold mysteries that are hidden in God. Moses was captured by God's vast love, gripped by the awesome, holy, majestic, splendor of His being, even though He was afraid and trembling (Hebrews 12:21). Moses approached God, trusting that he would not be destroyed. God called Moses up the mountain to meet with Him a number of times. Twice he stayed on the mountain for forty days and forty nights. After the second forty-day visitation, Moses had to put a veil over his face because the glory that was shining from him was too much for the Israelites to see (Exodus 34:33-35).

On other occasions, Moses met and spoke with the Lord face to face in a tent that was set up outside the Israelite camp. When he went to this tent of meeting the glory of God descended on the tent with such intensity that *all* the Israelites in the camp stood at the doors of their tents and worshiped God (Exodus 33:7-11). Moses loved the presence of God so much that he refused to lead the Israelites through the wilderness and into the promised land unless God's presence went with them (Exodus 33:15-17). In response to Moses' pleading God promised that His presence would go with them. Moses was still not satisfied and cried out for God to show him His full glory. Moses was permitted to behold God as He passed by. God's presence was so fiery that Moses was only permitted to see His back while sheltered behind a rock (Exodus 33:19-23).

Moses knew God more intimately than any other person on the face of the earth, and still he was not satisfied. To put this in context, think back to the time when God sent Moses to Egypt as a deliverer. At the word of Moses ten separate plagues of devastating proportions were released over the entire nation of Egypt. This is the only time in history that signs and wonders of this magnitude and extent were released through the ministry of a single man. Today many would do anything just to experience a small measure of the power and authority that was given to Moses. After being used by God like this, most people would be satisfied to sit back and remember. But for Moses, such power and authority could not compare to intimacy with God. Moses yearned to know the full embrace of God's covenant love – love that burns with fiery intensity.

THE BAPTISM OF FIRE

Under the Old Covenant, it was not possible to touch God. Sin separated God and man. But in New Testament times, God demonstrated His heart toward us by sending His only Son to earth to be given over to a cruel and merciless death. Jesus' death on the cross opened a door into God's immediate presence. Under the New Covenant the wall of separation was removed, causing God to break out and touch man with His presence. Not only can we touch Him but He also offers to completely immerse and saturate us with the Holy Spirit's presence, power and reality. Now we can come boldly and freely – yet so few do.

> Of this salvation the prophets have inquired and searched carefully, who prophesied of the grace that would come to you, searching what, or what manner of time, the Spirit of Christ who was in them was indicating when He testified beforehand the sufferings of Christ and the glories that would follow. To them it was revealed that, not to themselves, but to us they were ministering the things which now have been reported to you through those who have preached the gospel to you by the Holy Spirit sent from heaven – things which angels desire to look into (1 Peter 1:9-12).

The glory of the New Covenant is greater than that of the Old Covenant. Hebrews 12:18-29 says that we have been called not to Mount Sinai, speaking of Moses and the Old Covenant, but to Mount Zion, a heavenly mountain representing the New Covenant. Under the Old Covenant, God spoke to Moses from Mount Sinai. Today God is still speaking but now, through His Son, He speaks to us directly.

The Old Covenant given to Moses was glorious but the New Covenant spoken through Jesus is much more glorious (2 Corinthians 3:7-18). The writer of Hebrews warns: 'See that you do not refuse Him who speaks. For if they did not escape who refused Him who spoke on earth, much more shall we not escape if we turn away from Him who speaks from heaven… For our God is a consuming fire' (Hebrews 12:25, 29). Consider what Paul says about the New Covenant in 2 Corinthians 3.

> But if the ministry of death, written and engraved on stones, *was glorious*, so that the children of Israel could not look steadily at the face of Moses *because of the glory* of his countenance, which glory was passing away, how will the ministry of the Spirit *not be more glorious*? For if the ministry of condemnation *had glory*, the ministry of righteousness *exceeds much more in glory*. For even what was *made glorious* had no glory in this respect, because of *the glory that excels*. For if what is passing away *was glorious*, what remains is *much more glorious*. Now the Lord is the Spirit; and where the Spirit of the Lord is, there is liberty. But we all, with unveiled face, beholding as in a mirror *the glory* of the Lord, are being transformed into the same image *from glory to glory*, just as by the Spirit of the Lord. (2 Corinthians 3:7-11, 17-18. Emphasis added).

Paul makes it clear that in Christ the veil that separates us from God's glory is removed (2 Corinthians 3:12-16). Which makes us ask, 'Where is the glory?' If this glorious inheritance is available to us today how do we obtain it?

The Invitation

John the Baptist was a forerunner who prepared the way for Jesus. His ministry was an invitation to 'behold the Lamb of God' (John 1:29). His call for repentance, in preparation for the coming Kingdom, was a prophetic invitation for people to know God. As the forerunner of Christ, the words he spoke about Him are of great importance. He said in Matthew 3:11-12, 'I indeed baptize you with water unto repentance, but He who is coming after me is mightier than I, whose sandals I am not worthy to carry. He will baptize you with the Holy Spirit and fire. His winnowing fan is in His hand, and He will thoroughly clean out His threshing floor, and gather His wheat into the barn; but He will burn up the chaff with unquenchable fire.'

In these verses John says three things about Jesus:

1. He is mighty. I am not even worthy to carry His sandals.

2. He will baptize you with the Holy Spirit and fire.

3. He will separate the wheat from the chaff. The wheat will be gathered and the chaff burned.

The first statement is about who Jesus is. The second and third tell us what He will do. These three things could be summarized as follows:

1. Jesus is God.

2. He comes to bring us into an experiential relationship with Himself.

3. Whether you enter into or reject His invitation will determine your eternal destiny.

The baptism of the Holy Spirit and fire that John the Baptist declared is of utmost importance. Bible commentators are divided over whether the fire Jesus mentions in Matthew 3:11 is related to the baptism of the Holy Spirit or the judgment spoken of in the following verse. No matter what Jesus meant, we know that 'God is a consuming fire' (Hebrews 12:29) and that the Holy Spirit is God (2 Corinthians 3:17). With this in mind, I will refer to fire as an aspect of the baptism of the Holy Spirit.

The word 'baptize' means to completely immerse. Jesus comes not just to touch us with the Spirit and fire but to completely immerse us. The Holy Spirit is a powerful person. When God spoke in the beginning, it was the Holy Spirit who caused creation to come into being. He is also the one who searches out the depths of God. To be saturated and surrounded in His presence is an awesome experience and could be likened to being immersed in fire. To put only your hand into fire is a powerful experience!

Fire is intense and it consumes. God's love is so intense it burns the same way. Fire changes things. The baptism of the Holy Spirit is not a little goose bump, making us feel good, as many have been led to believe. Paul says in Ephesians 5:18-21, 'And do not be drunk with wine, in which is dissipation; but be filled with the Spirit, speaking to one another in psalms and hymns and spiritual songs, singing and making melody in your heart to the Lord, giving thanks always for all things to God the Father in the name of our Lord Jesus Christ, submitting to one another in the fear of God.'

The word 'filled' is used in a continuous tense, meaning that we are to be repeatedly and continually filled with the Spirit. A person filled with the Spirit will spontaneously do the things described in verses 19, 20 and 21. The baptism of the Holy Spirit is not an end, it is a beginning. It is a holy encounter, causing us to enter into a living, dynamic relationship with God. We are not to be filled once but continuously. Our God is an extravagant, lavish God. He is not stingy and cheap. He is eternal, infinite and unlimited.

John the Baptist baptized 'with water unto repentance'. Repentance is simply the act of turning from sin in order to enter into a new life. The Israelites had extremely high standards of morality. John's preaching exposed sin even at a subconscious heart level. Repentance is to turn from and forsake our familiar life of sin so we can have something much better. God wants us to know Him. John the Baptist simply turned people in the right direction so that they could come into a much greater experience of God. He never gave them that experience but pointed to the One (Jesus) who could give it. It is Jesus who baptizes with the Holy Spirit and fire. John the Baptist himself never experienced this. That is why Matthew 11:11 says, 'Assuredly, I say to you, among those born of women there has not risen one greater than John the Baptist; but he who is least in the kingdom of heaven is greater than he.'

We have to be aware of what baptism with the Holy Spirit and fire will do. 'His winnowing fan is in His hand, and He will thoroughly clean out His threshing floor, and gather His wheat into the barn; but He will burn up the chaff with unquenchable fire' (Matthew 3:12). A winnowing fan was used to separate the wheat from the chaff. It was used to throw the wheat into the air so the wind could blow away the chaff. Wind in the Bible is often symbolic of the Holy Spirit. His first name is holy. When He comes He causes things that are not like Him to be removed. He will 'thoroughly purge His threshing floor'. Just like fire purges what is combustible, so His fire purges that which is unholy. The wheat that will be gathered is that which has His likeness stamped on it, that which has been fire-branded by God Himself.

A God You Can Experience

Christianity is experiential. Throughout eternity the Father, the Son and the Holy Spirit have lived in deep, intimate fellowship with each other. John bears witness to this when he says, 'In the beginning was the Word, the Word was with God, and the Word was God' (John 1:1). The phrase 'the Word was *with* God' can also be translated 'the Word was *toward* God'. The Father and the Son were face to face in a relationship of such depth and intimacy that nothing was held back or hidden from the other. If every relationship of intimacy on earth were added up, the result would barely register compared to the relationship between the Father and the Son. God created man to share in the glory of this relationship. This truth is foundational to true, biblical Christianity.

When Jesus was asked which commandment is the greatest, He responded by saying, '"You shall love the Lord your God with all your heart, with all your soul, and with all your mind." This is the first and great commandment. And the second is like it: "You shall love your neighbor as yourself." On these two commandments hang all the Law and the Prophets' (Matthew 22:37-40).

These two commands are *relational* and *experiential*. It is possible to live by the laws, principles, exhortation and wisdom of scripture and still not have an experiential knowledge of God Himself. Even non-

Christians can live by the principles of Scripture and be better off. It may be wise to live by God's laws but if that is all we settle for, we have missed the most important and vital part of what God offers.

Despite the fact that life is a continual sequence of experiences, many think that when it comes to God He is too distant to experience. This way of thinking says that faith is necessary because God is not tangible. There *are* seasons in which we hang on in faith even though we feel completely void of the reality of God, but this does not mean that faith and experience are mutually exclusive. There are also seasons in the Christian life when the firsthand experience of the reality of God causes our faith to expand. This faith is then tested during the dry seasons. But despite this, for many Christians, faith means relating to a God they cannot experience.

Another group of Christians believe that relationship with God is experiential but they place a limit on how much we can experience. James 4:8 says, 'Draw near to God and He will draw near to you.' In other words, we can be as close to God as we choose to be. What a person gets out of life is largely determined by their own choices. Some choose to live a life of shallow experiences, too frightened to relate deeply with others; too frightened to look into someone else's eyes in case they might experience more emotion than they are prepared for; too frightened to let anyone see into their heart in case they become overwhelmed with shame or vulnerability.

Our experience is related to our capacity to meet heart to heart with others. Our capacity to meet is determined by our willingness to be vulnerable. It's easy to pass others by as we go about life; it's not so easy to stop and look someone in the eye and see the hurt, the pain and the loneliness in their heart. Matthew 6:22 says, 'The lamp of the body is the eye.' We see pictures of hungry starving children on posters or on our television screens, but how different it would be to look one of those children in the eye. Suddenly we would feel some of the pain and anguish they have experienced. In the same way, God wants us to be able to look into His eyes and intimately know His heart, and let Him do the same to us.

Amos 3:7 says, 'Surely the Lord God does nothing, unless He reveals

His secret to His servants the prophets.' The word 'secret' here means 'counsel' (a company of people in close deliberation) and has the implication of intimacy, consultation, a shared secret.[1] It speaks of the counsel of the Godhead. A true prophet is someone who lives so close to God that He knows the intimate thoughts, feelings, plans and secrets of the Godhead.

In Revelation chapter one, the apostle John described the eyes of Jesus as a flame of fire, His voice like the sound of many waters (Revelation 1:14-15). Two of our primary ways of communicating are our eyes and our voice. The experience was so overwhelming for John that he fell down like a dead man at the feet of Jesus. If we could observe the interaction of the Godhead it would, like John, short-circuit us, and yet ultimately we are called to enter into this fellowship.

A New Way of Life

When Jesus arrived on the scene He proclaimed a way of life that was radically different from anything anyone had known before. The incredible thing about Jesus' command for us to love God is the extent and degree to which this love is to be expressed – 'with all your heart, with all your soul, with all your mind and with all your strength' – in other words, it should be intense, passionate and focused. If the things we do in life do not increase our love for God and for one another then we must question whether we are truly living as God would have us live. Jesus said that we would do greater works than He did (John 14:12). What was the secret of Jesus works? 'The Father who dwells in Me does the works' (John 14:10). The secret to doing the works of Jesus and even greater works is a deep, intimate, abiding relationship with Father God. This style of life was demonstrated by Jesus Himself.

Man Shall Not Live by Bread Alone

> Then Jesus was led up by the Spirit into the wilderness to be tempted by the devil. And when He had fasted forty days and forty nights, afterward He was hungry. Now when the tempter came to Him, he

said, 'If You are the Son of God, command that these stones become bread.' But He answered and said, 'It is written, "Man shall not live by bread alone, but by every word that proceeds from the mouth of God"' (Matthew 4:1-4).

The maximum period it is advisable to fast is forty days – after forty days the body starts burning up muscle tissue, resulting in intense hunger. It was while Jesus was in this state of intense hunger that the devil chose to come and tempt Him. Jesus' response showed that His love for His Father was greater than the intense hunger he was experiencing. Jesus literally lived by every word that was proceeding (present, continuous tense) from the mouth of the Father. Jesus' heart toward His Father is expressed in the following modern worship song called 'Breathe'.

This is the air I breathe
This is the air I breathe
Your holy presence living in me

This is my daily bread
This is my daily bread
Your very word spoken to me

And I, I'm desperate for You
And I, I'm lost without You[2]

Before Jesus was tempted by the devil the Father spoke in an audible voice: 'And suddenly a voice came from heaven, saying, "This is My beloved Son, in whom I am well pleased"' (Matthew 3:17).

Love is expressed through communication. The Father expressed His love and affirmation for Jesus. Jesus did not start His ministry until after the temptation, and the Father had spoken His affirmation before that. So Jesus knew that He was pleasing to the Father *before* He started His earthly ministry. It is extremely important to minister to the Father and let Him minister to us *before* we enter into our earthly ministries. Those who get this process the wrong way round end up ministering in order to please the Father rather than ministering out of a relationship with the Father. A loving relationship with Father God causes us to know His pleasure and delight in us without us having to do anything to earn it. God is not after our actions, He is after us.

Jesus prayed that we would have the same love that He and the Father have for each other, 'And the glory which You gave Me I have given them, that they may be one just as We are one' (John 17:22). This prayer will be answered. The purpose of the covenant is to bring us into 'oneness'. We shouldn't be satisfied with anything less.

A Shocking Warning

Jesus gives a shocking warning in Matthew 7:21-23: 'Not everyone who says to Me, "Lord, Lord," shall enter the kingdom of heaven, but he who does the will of My Father in heaven. Many will say to Me in that day, "Lord, Lord, have we not prophesied in Your name, cast out demons in Your name, and done many wonders in Your name?" And then I will declare to them, "I never knew you; depart from Me, you who practise lawlessness!"'

Many will come before the Lord at the end of time, believing that prophesying, casting out demons and performing signs and wonders will prove that they know Him and have made Him Lord of their lives. These actions cannot be done without the Holy Spirit. But Jesus declared, 'I never knew you.' In Revelation 3 Jesus rebuked the church at Ephesus for exalting the work of God above their first love relationship with Him, adding that unless they repented He would remove their 'lampstand' from before Him.

It is one thing to let the Spirit do something through you and another to let Him permeate your innermost being (baptize you), placing the stamp of His nature and likeness on you, and letting Him thoroughly purge you of anything unholy. When Jesus said, 'I never knew you', the word 'know' does not mean merely recognition. It means to know through experience by 'an active relation between the one who knows and the person or thing known'.[3] It is not just knowing *about* someone, but coming to know or entering into familiarity through personal interaction.

It is usually gained through personal acquaintance or some relationship of intimacy.[4] This word 'know' is used extensively throughout the New Testament. One example of its use is found in 1 John 4:16, 'And we have *known* and believed the love that God has for us' (italics mine). So deep is the interaction of this love that John goes on to say, 'God is love and he who abides in love abides in God, and God in him.'

The Early Church

The thing that set the early Church apart from the world was their first-hand experience. Only some Christians had witnessed Jesus' resurrection from the dead by physically seeing Him, but they could all witness to the power and reality of the resurrected Christ after He ascended to heaven. They tasted this resurrection life themselves, causing them to be witnesses of the resurrection. This formed the basis of the testimony by which they were able to overcome Satan. 'And they overcame him by the blood of the Lamb and by the word of their testimony, and they did not love their lives to the death' (Revelation 12:11). The testimony referred to here is the testimony of their experience of God. John elaborates on this in 1 John 1:1-4:

> That which was from the beginning, which we have heard, which we have seen with our eyes, which we have looked upon, and our hands have handled, concerning the Word of life – the life was manifested, and we have seen, and bear witness, and declare to you that eternal life which was with the Father and was manifested to us – that which we have seen and heard we declare to you, that you also may have fellowship with us; and truly our fellowship is with the Father and with His Son Jesus Christ. And these things we write to you that your joy may be full.

Paul's Love for God

Paul earnestly desired to know the love of God. In Ephesians 1:17 he prayed concerning the Ephesian Christians, 'That the God of our Lord

Jesus Christ, the Father of glory, may give to you the spirit of wisdom and revelation in the knowledge of Him.' We can only know the love of God by revelation. God is willing to give this revelation to all who ask for it. When we pray for others, He is also willing to reveal His love to them. God wants us to draw close to Him so that He can share the mysteries and secrets of His heart – things so deep and intimate that man is not permitted to utter them (2 Corinthians 12:4). Paul's prayer was that every Christian would come to know the full glory of God's love for us – 'that Christ may dwell in your hearts through faith; that you, being rooted and grounded in love, may be able to comprehend with all the saints what is the width and length and depth and height – to know the love of Christ which passes knowledge; that you may be filled with all the fullness of God' (Ephesians 3:17-19). The Amplified Bible expresses verse 19 more emphatically; '[That you may really come] to know [practically, through experience for yourselves] the love of Christ, which far surpasses mere knowledge [without experience]; that you may be filled [through all your being] unto all the fullness of God [may have the richest measure of the divine Presence, and become a body wholly filled and flooded with God Himself!]' (Ephesians 3:19 AMP).

Paul's letter to the Ephesians is applicable to the wider body of Christ. But it must be stressed that the church at Ephesus was the primary recipient. Paul had been based at this church for over two years. During this time, Ephesus experienced an incredible visitation of God. Special miracles were carried out at the hands of Paul, and the word of God spread to all of Asia. Despite this awesome demonstration of God's power, Paul still prays that Christ may dwell in their hearts through faith. Paul is not referring to Christ coming into our hearts at salvation. Nor is he praying merely for a demonstration of God's power. He is praying for something much more. As Jesus said in John 14:23, 'If anyone loves Me, he will keep My word; and My Father will love him, and We will come to him and make Our home with him.'

The Deep and Intimate Knowledge of God

Paul instructed Timothy in 1 Timothy 1:5, 'Now the purpose of the commandment is love' and again in 1 Corinthians 14:1 Paul's command to the Corinthians was to pursue love.

The more Paul came to experience God's love the more he realized how little he knew. Paul's desire to personally know God's love increased throughout his life. There is a subtle pride that can creep into our lives when we think that we know God. Towards the end of Paul's life he penned the following words,

> Yes, furthermore, I count everything as loss compared to the possession of the priceless privilege [the overwhelming preciousness, the surpassing worth, and supreme advantage] of knowing Christ Jesus my Lord and of progressively becoming more deeply and intimately acquainted with Him [of perceiving and recognizing and understanding Him more fully and clearly]. For His sake I have lost everything and consider it all to be mere rubbish (refuse, dregs), in order that I may win (gain) Christ (the Anointed one). [For my determined purpose is] that I may know Him [that I may progressively become more deeply and intimately acquainted with Him, perceiving and recognizing and understanding the wonders of His Person more strongly and more clearly] (Philippians 3:8,10a AMP).

The love of God is so great that even Paul, after experiencing and knowing God for years, cried out toward the end of His life, 'That I may know Him.' What we need most in our generation is for the knowledge of God's love to reach beyond our minds so that it can touch and impact our hearts.

Bungee Jumping

Over the last twenty years a new adventure sport has become popular in New Zealand. It's called 'bungee jumping'. This involves jumping from a bridge over a deep gorge. The only thing that keeps you from plummeting into the river below is an elastic rubber cord tied around your ankles. I like watching others jump, but I've never wanted to do it myself. Many people need a lot of coaxing to finally take the plunge. This is similar to delving into the knowledge of God. Consider what Paul has to say in 1 Corinthians 2:9-10 (AMP):

> But, on the contrary, as the Scripture says, What eye has not seen and ear has not heard and has not entered into the heart of man, [all that] God has prepared (made and keeps ready) for those who love Him [who hold Him in affectionate reverence, promptly obeying Him and gratefully recognizing the benefits He has bestowed]. Yet to us God has unveiled and revealed them by and through His Spirit, for the [Holy] Spirit searches diligently, exploring and examining everything, even sounding the profound and bottomless things of God [the divine counsels and things hidden and beyond man's scrutiny].

The Message paraphrase of the Bible translates verse 10, 'The Spirit, not content to flit around on the surface, dives into the depths of God.'

So how deep is deep? Since it is the Holy Spirit who reveals the depth of God let us consider some of His characteristics.

The Holy Spirit reveals the love of God to us (Romans 5:5). His love is spontaneous and free. It is impossible to try to be loving. The only way that we can obey the command of Jesus to love God with all our heart, soul, mind and strength is to know the intensity of God's love for us. The more we understand God's love, the more we are able to respond to it. The enemy has worked hard to cut us off from the inheritance past on to us from our spiritual forebears. He has also cajoled us into thinking we understand and know the love of God, causing our perception of God's love to be stunted. But our God is limitless, His love unending, inexpressible and indefinable. Consider the words of this poem,

> Your love colors the dawn
> Your voice the power of thunder
> Your hand the healer of the weak
> Your love fills oceans and Your voice calms the seas
> And You created me
> Your eyes are so amazing, so deep
> Like crashing waves on a cloudy sea

> And these pounding waves they consume me
> But there's so much more to You, so much I do not know
> So much love I have not yet encountered
> So much You overflow
> And just when I think I know Your complexities You step into the light
> And just when I think I know Your voice You open up my ears
> It's like trying to know every single glowing star on a cloudless night
> But Your depth and Your vastness keep me running after You.[5]

The Holy Spirit is real, deep and unlimited. He wants us to learn to let go and trust Him as He takes us into the depths of God. 'Now the Lord is the Spirit; and where the Spirit of the Lord is, there is liberty' (2 Corinthians 3:17). 'And all of us, as with unveiled face, [because we] continued to behold [in the Word of God] as in a mirror the glory of the Lord, are constantly being transfigured into His very own image in ever increasing splendor and from one degree of glory to another; [for this comes] from the Lord [Who is the] Spirit' (2 Corinthians 3:18 AMP).

The Holy Spirit is Lord. It has often been said that He is either Lord of all or not Lord at all. What stops us from making Him Lord of all? Just like someone preparing to bungee jump off a bridge, we must overcome our fear and take the leap.

Are you ready to make the jump? It is time to move beyond just scratching the surface of who God is and continue the legacy of passion that has been left to us. God is still calling for men and women to pursue Him with reckless abandon. He is about to touch a generation with the intense fire of His love and invite them into fellowship with Him. This invitation is open to everyone from the least to the greatest. It is time to heed the call and seek Him with all of our hearts.

Holy Spirit, we want to dive into the depths of God with the same reckless abandon that you have. Help us to overcome fear and shame. Take our trembling hands and give us courage as You lead us into the deep and intimate knowledge of God.

Part 3:

OBSTACLES THAT KEEP US FROM THE SECRET PLACE

THE SECRET PLACE

In the depths of every human heart there is a desperate longing to know a place of hidden, unparalleled beauty. This secret place is where our interaction with God takes place, where we know that we are specially and uniquely His. It is a place where we delight God in a way that no other person can delight Him because we are unique.

Every snowflake is different, but to the naked eye they all look the same. A magnifying glass reveals patterns in each one that are intricate and beautiful. Every snowflake hides its own unique secrets that are only visible under magnification. Likewise every human carries unique secrets. Some of these secrets are visible to others who truly and genuinely love us, but some of them are only visible to God. Just like a married couple have an intimacy that only they share, so every child of God is called to have an intimacy with Him. The lyrics to the following song express the yearning of a child hungry for the love of God:

Deep down inside
Inside my soul I feel passion and fire
I've got a yearning that words cannot express
A hunger for love and tenderness

Deep down inside
I know you feel the hunger and so do I
When the wonder of a fairy tale will never fail

There must be a place
Where dreams come true

> There must be a time
> When I'm free to fly
> There must be a place
>
> Deep down inside
> Inside my heart I'm falling one more time
> Overtaken by the promise of love
> That I have been made a captive of
>
> Deep down inside
> I'd do anything if only I could find
> Find all the memories of once upon a time
> I want to make them mine
>
> There must be something inside of me
> That keeps believing in love
> What is this something inside of me
> That knows there's so much more
> Makes it all worth living for[1]

What keeps us from that secret place? In exploring this subject it is easy to be left with a sense of complete bewilderment about how we can ever meet with God at this level. It seems so 'out there' that we find it hard to believe it's real. The very thought of connecting with an awesome, holy God can be hard to grasp. 'When I pray I don't feel or sense anything – in fact, it feels like I'm talking to thin air.' Why is it many feel that the closest thing to their prayer life is the hot, dry barrenness of the Sahara desert, or the bitter cold of the Antarctic? Why is it that for some, prayer is as engaging as eating a plate of dry bran?

Knowing and interacting closely with God through devotional prayer is only possible after various obstacles have been removed. Here are some important questions that need to be addressed in order to overcome the obstacles that stand in the way of intimacy with God:

Is God interested in me personally?

Whose approval do we seek – God or man's?
How do you abide in the secret place?
Am I worthy to have an intimate relationship with God?
How much emotion is enough?
What processes does God use to draw us closer to Him?

Is God Really Interested in Me?

Around the time the face of Jesus appeared on the wall in Vanuatu, the Lord taught us many things. During the day Joy had told the Lord she would spend some time with Him that evening. She thought no more about it as she was overtaken by the busyness of the day. That night, just as she was dozing off to sleep, she felt someone pull her finger. Her husband, Raynold, was asleep and there was no one else in the room. Suddenly she remembered her promise about spending time with God. She had forgotten, but God had not and had come to give her a gentle reminder. God waits in anticipation for us to meet with Him.

One of the main reasons many never persevere with devotional prayer, or religiously continue in it without drawing closer to God, is because they fail to understand God's response towards them when they seek His face. God longs to hear the voice of His people. If we fail to understand that fact, our prayers become ritualistic, something done out of duty rather than desire for Him. Song of Solomon 2:14 says; 'O my dove, in the clefts of the rock, in the secret places of the cliff, let me see your face, let me hear your voice; for your voice is sweet, and your face is lovely.'

God, like any other lover, wants to hear your voice. He sees past imperfections, straight into the heart where He notices our tentative desire to turn toward Him. This blesses Him so much that He says over and over again, 'Let Me hear your voice.' Aside from the words we use, God just loves to hear our voice. He misses it when we don't speak and commune with Him. Sometimes, we can become so focused on having a method of prayer or a string of requests and petitions, we forget that prayer primarily involves the language of love.

I can remember a particularly devastating season in my own life. I would come to God in prayer, as I had always done, but would find I had nothing to say. I was too hurt, too devastated, too broken to speak. This lasted for several months. It is the only time in my life that I lived to sleep. I literally couldn't wait to fall asleep each night so that I could escape from feeling the way I was. Despite all of this I continued to come before God in prayer, although I simply sat in silence.

Despite my silence it helped to just come before Him, knowing that He saw me and knew my heart, and was pleased that I was there. It wasn't long after this time that I went on the mission trip to Vanuatu and saw the face of Jesus on the wall. I had gone from one extreme to the other. For a long time it had felt like God was not near, although I knew He was. Next thing, I was thrust into the reality of God being so close it was truly mind-blowing. God never changes. He is the same yesterday, today and tomorrow. His love towards us is as great in the times He seems far away as in the times His tangible presence is strong. No matter what the situation, God wants to hear our voices. In fact, it means more to Him when He hears our voices and expressions of love during the dry wilderness seasons of life.

The Song of Solomon is full of the imagery and language of love. This book has long been considered as a metaphor of love between Christ and His Bride. The words of Song of Solomon 2:14 come after a section where the Lover (Jesus) has been exhorting the Shulamite woman to rise up and come away with Him. Finally, expressing His deepest longing, He calls out to her. More than just a casual suggestion, this verse expresses the cry of one overwhelmed with love.

'O my dove'

Earlier in Song of Solomon (1:15) the Lover says that the Shulamite has dove's eyes. The dove is the only bird that can focus both eyes on one object. In saying that she has dove's eyes, He is extolling the fact that she has begun to notice Him above all else. One of my constant prayers is, 'Give me eyes for only You.' When we focus on God, when we draw aside to look on His face, He comes to us and says, 'You have dove's eyes.' The Shulamite had begun to taste His goodness, but her commitment to Him was still superficial and tentative. She is yet to be completely won over by His love. However, He sees her desire to be completely His, and this causes Him to praise her for her eyes of love.

In Song of Solomon 2:14, the Lover not only says that she has dove's eyes but also likens her to a dove. In poetic language doves are a beautiful and powerful metaphor for the language and expression of love. The following things can be noted about doves:

1. They appear to express affection for each other by stroking each other, 'billing and cooing'.

2. They have soft eyes. By calling the Shulamite his dove, He is saying, 'You have eyes of love – soft, gentle and tender.' He is calling her to come away with Him and be like a dove in its expression of affection and intimacy.

3. They are used as a symbol of innocence and singleness of devotion; they have only one partner and mate for life.

4. They share the nesting and parenting duties. By this He is acknowledging her desirability as a partner to work alongside Him, bringing forth offspring that carry and bear His image.

5. Doves are gentle and never resist an attack or retaliate against enemies. This speaks of both the gentleness and vulnerability of love. He knows she is fragile and delicate. By calling her 'My dove', He lays claim to her, offering to protect and nurture her in her frail and vulnerable state.

'In the clefts of the rock, in the secret places of the cliff'

Doves nest in lofty cliffs and deep ravines. Because they are timid and non-aggressive, crags provide a place of protection and safety where they can rest, away from their enemies. This verse shows that the Shulamite is hiding from her lover. She is not ready to be vulnerable and open – overburdened with fear, she is tentative to show her face.

'Let me see your countenance'

Jesus longs to be able to look on us. He calls us out of our hiding places to come and be face to face with Him. A major reason we hide is because we feel undesirable. Full of shame and condemnation, we hide from His face. The Accuser of the Brethren (Satan) continually reminds us of our shortcomings and failures, but he also goes as far as to say that there is nothing desirable in us. This is one of the biggest lies of the enemy. God Himself says we are wonderfully and fearfully made, made in His very image (Psalm 139:14, Genesis 1:27). There is nothing you can do, no matter how bad, that can change this fact. As long as you have life and breath, He will continue to pursue you as someone who has such worth to Him that He died for you. The Lord pleads with us not to let condemnation and shame cause us to hide our faces from Him.

Throughout the rest of the Song of Solomon, the Lover continues to affirm how beautiful the Shulamite is in every aspect of her countenance. If we would listen to God's voice, we would hear Him say exactly the same about us. He sees beyond what is marred by sin to that which is created in His image. You reveal an aspect of God that no one else can. God searches for us with great determination and patience. He continually affirms us as an incredible piece of handwork, made by the greatest Artist of all and written all over with His signature. He continues to affirm us even though we find it hard to believe that what He says about us and what He sees in us are actually true.

After the Shulamite was continually affirmed for her beauty, she was able to slowly but surely come out of hiding and give herself completely to the Lover of her soul. Stop listening to the Accuser of the Brethren and hear for yourself the voice of the One who speaks not the language of accusation but rather the language of love.

'Let me hear your voice'

Concerning the voice of the Lord, David says in Psalm 29:3-9:

> The voice of the Lord is over the waters;

The God of glory thunders;
The Lord is over many waters.
The voice of the Lord is powerful;
The voice of the Lord is full of majesty.
The voice of the Lord breaks the cedars,
Yes, the Lord splinters the cedars of Lebanon.
He makes them also skip like a calf,
Lebanon and Sirion like a young wild ox.
The voice of the Lord divides the flames of fire.
The voice of the Lord shakes the wilderness;
The Lord shakes the Wilderness of Kadesh.
The voice of the Lord makes the deer give birth,
And strips the forests bare;
And in His temple everyone says, 'Glory!'

John says in the book of Revelation that when he heard the Lord speak it was like a trumpet (Revelation 1:10) and that it sounded like the voice of multitudes of rushing waters (Revelation 1:15). The overwhelming power and majesty of God's voice reveals something of the unfathomable depth and power of who He is. Incredible as it may seem He longs to hear *our* voices. Why?

'For your voice is sweet, and your countenance is lovely'

It is impossible, with our limited comprehension, to understand why God loves us. In our pursuit of Jesus we need to realize that He too pursues us with unrelenting passion. He wants to draw us in until we know His resplendent countenance, His eyes of fire, and His powerful voice. When we know that He longs to see us and hear us, prayer no longer seems irrelevant and boring. Even in the dry, barren seasons of life, God delights in hearing our voices. Even though we are fearful and immature, He sees the desire of our hearts toward Him and responds, 'You have dove's eyes.'

Whose Approval Do You Seek?

Knowing that God desires to hear our voices is the starting point for intimacy with Him. But prayer is more than just an initial meeting place. Our interaction with Him is a journey.

> And when you pray, you shall not be like the hypocrites. For they love to pray standing in the synagogues and on the corners of the streets, that they may be seen by men. Assuredly, I say to you, they have their reward. But you, when you pray, go into your room, and when you have shut your door, pray to your Father who is in the secret place; and your Father who sees in secret will reward you openly (Matthew 6:5-6).

This passage speaks of two types of pray-ers. The first are those who pray before other people and the second are those who pray before God. We shall call them people pray-ers and God pray-ers. People pray-ers are people pleasers – those who always have to prove themselves to others. Because of their feelings of inferiority or insecurity, they have a need to be seen to be performing well, and to appear to have everything together in their lives. They need to look good on the outside. People pray-ers cover up and deny how they really feel on the inside by setting up an external façade. They are not only concerned with measuring up and looking good in the eyes of others, they also try frantically to measure up to their own high expectations as well as the expectations they believe God puts on them.

People pray-ers fall into two categories: those who are more obviously proud and believe that they are able to impress others, and those who have given up believing that they are able to impress anyone, particularly God. The second category is a much more subtle form of pride. These people are unable to step out and participate, for example, in a public prayer meeting for fear that their prayers are not good enough or anointed enough.

Always comparing ourselves with others, or putting ourselves down for not measuring up, shows that we are people pray-ers controlled by what others think of us. People pray-ers have one basic problem – they are not able to rest in God's love for them.

God pray-ers, on the other hand, *are* able to rest in God's love for them. They know that He delights in them and favors them simply because they are His children.

God loves us because we are His, not because we perform to a certain standard. All of us are on a journey from being people pray-ers who strive for love and acceptance to becoming God pray-ers who are able to rest in God's unconditional love. Prayer is not some rigorous, torturous discipline only obtained by a few noble souls. Rather it is the natural, often spontaneous interaction between a father and a child. True, our flesh-nature hates to pray, but the joy of prayer is knowing that we are loved and that our heavenly Father delights in us.

How Do You Abide in the Secret Place?

> I am the true vine, and My Father is the vinedresser. Every branch in Me that does not bear fruit He takes away; and every branch that bears fruit He prunes, that it may bear more fruit.
>
> You are already clean because of the word which I have spoken to you. Abide in Me, and I in you. As the branch cannot bear fruit of itself, unless it abides in the vine, neither can you, unless you abide in Me. I am the vine, you are the branches. He who abides in Me, and I in him, bears much fruit; for without Me you can do nothing. If anyone does not abide in Me, he is cast out as a branch and is withered; and they gather them and throw them into the fire, and they are burned. If you abide in Me, and My words abide in you, you will ask what you desire, and it shall be done for you. By this My Father is glorified, that you bear much fruit; so you will be My disciples (John 15:1-8).

When we abide in Jesus, we are lovingly tended by the Father who is the 'vinedresser'. *Strong's Concordance* defines 'meno', the Greek word for abide as 'to stay (in a given place, state, relation or expectancy)'.[2] Abiding involves four things:

1. *Staying in a given place – the secret place.* The more we develop a secret relationship with the Father, the more we are able to carry that relationship into every situation and circumstance we face. By 'secret', I mean intimate and sacred. During World War II, Corrie ten Boon was sent to a concentration camp because her family sheltered Jews from the German forces that had invaded Holland. She spoke of how it was her relationship with her father that helped her through this difficult time. As Corrie was growing up, she vividly remembered how every night her father would come and say goodnight to her. After tucking her into bed and praying a short prayer, he would lay his hand on her and say, 'I love you, Corrie.' As her father left the room, Corrie would lie motionless so that it felt as though her father's hand was still on her as she drifted off to sleep. Her father's hand gave her a sense of security. In the concentration camps each night as she went to sleep, she would feel her father's hand touch her and say, 'I love you, Corrie', only this time it was the hand of her heavenly Father. Although Corrie was separated from her natural father, she was still able to carry her bond with him into the horrific experience of existing in concentration camps. A secret relationship cannot be robbed from you. The more you experience it, the greater the impact it has on the whole of your life.

2. *Staying in a given state.* A married couple express their love for each other in the privacy (or secret place) of their home. As they go in their separate directions each day, they carry the reality of that secret relationship with them. In a sense, they are with each other, in their hearts. So it is with our relationship with Father God. Wherever we go, He is actually there. There are times when we shut everything else out and express our love fully, but more and more we learn to abide in this secret place at all times. To abide in this state involves humility and trust. 'God resists the proud, but gives grace to the humble' (James 4:6).

Pride causes our relationship with God to be severed in much the same way that a rift exists between a husband and wife after they have had an argument. Only the humility of asking forgiveness and trusting your heart once again to the one who has hurt you can open the door to intimacy. It is the same in our relationship with God. Even though He is perfectly loving and kind, we often blame Him for the negative experiences of life. We reason that He, being God, should be able to prevent such things from happening. He is, after all, omnipresent, omniscient and omnipotent. God, however, gave authority over the earth to Adam and Eve. Through sin Satan has been able to usurp this authority. In a sense humans still have authority over the earth but by opening themselves up to sin, they invite Satan to come and have control. Conversely, by opening up to righteousness and yielding to God, our authority to rule over the earth is restored. God only intervenes if He has been invited and He will never violate the free will of mankind.

God is not to blame for tragedy. Sin reaps death and destruction. Even when God releases His judgment because of sin, it is only after repeated warnings and earnest pleas to return to Him. Because we live in a sinful, fallen world we have to deal with the tragedy and death that surrounds us. However, we must be careful not to harden our hearts toward God as though He were to blame. Such hardness of heart stops us from abiding in the vine.

We need to ask God to forgive us for hardening our hearts toward Him. God is not always who we think He is. The devil tries to make us believe that God is a tyrant that cannot be trusted. 'For thus says the Lord God, the Holy One of Israel: "In returning and rest you shall be saved; In quietness and confidence shall be your strength." But you would not' (Isaiah 30:15). Anger at God does not bring about 'returning and rest'. Mistrust does not bring about 'quietness and confidence'. God continually calls us to a state of humility, dependence and trust so that we can abide in Him.

3. *Staying in a given relationship.* It goes without saying that to have a relationship you have to relate. To relate involves time, and because we live in a fallen world, it also involves determination to remove the obstacles that continually come between us and other people. Many find it hard to spend time with God and give up after a few days. I recommend starting small – say five or ten minutes a day. Spiritual disciplines are built up little by little. You don't go out and instantly run a marathon without building up your strength and stamina. As you keep your appointment

with God, it becomes easier. Relationships don't start straight away. They have to be built over time. It takes at least a month to establish a habit, so it is best to commit to something you know you will be able to keep.

If you were not related to in an open, safe and trusting environment when you were a child then relationships can become an unpleasant and awkward experience rather than a pleasant and natural one. Sunflowers open up and bloom in direct sunlight. In the same way, our hearts are only able to open up and reflect God's glory when we focus on His love for us.

God made the human heart sensitive so that we could relate to Him and others. But because it is sensitive, it is also easily wounded. God, however, is more patient than we can ever understand. He loves it when we bring our wounded hearts to Him. Having a relationship with God is not always easy because it exposes hidden pain in our hearts. Even though we would rather bury, forget and deny that pain, to stay in relationship with God we must understand that He is loving, gentle and kind and that He always has our best interests in mind.

4. *Staying in a state of expectancy toward Him.* 'Every good gift and every perfect gift is from above, and comes down from the Father of lights, with whom there is no variation or shadow of turning' (James 1:17). Human beings are changeable. Natural fathers are changeable but our heavenly Father never changes. He is consistent in His love for us. He isn't loving and kind one moment and hostile the next. God's actions are not always predictable but His character certainly is. When we come to the Father, He consistently rewards us. 'Blessed are those who hunger and thirst for righteousness, for they shall be filled' (Matthew 5:6). 'But without faith it is impossible to please Him, for he who comes to God must believe that He is, and that He is a rewarder of those who diligently seek Him' (Hebrews 11:6).

What is your expectation of God? Do you expect Him to abuse, mistreat or ignore you, or do you trust Him to pour His favor over your life?

Pruning

Finally, let us note that all who abide in the vine and become fruitful go through seasons of pruning. Pruning is not designed to punish or torment us, but rather so that we can become more fruitful. When vines are pruned, the branches are cut right back to the base. There are times when everything else is stripped away and we find ourselves running to the secret place with even greater fervor. The roots of our heart sink even deeper into God, giving us a stronger foundation so that we can carry more fruit. Too much fruit, too soon, can cause us to topple over with pride or be uprooted and separated from Him.

It is good to remember who the Pruner is. Some think they need to prune themselves and they cut away too little or too much, or simply in the wrong places. Some let the opinions or examples of others prune them and do not know the inner secrets of their own souls. But the only one who should prune is our loving heavenly Father, who is an expert pruner, and always and only prunes for our good.

There is no greater joy than when two people share a secret intimacy between them that nobody else knows. God is waiting and longing to keep the appointment with you.

THE GREAT DECEPTION

Christian songwriter Evan Earwicker writes about the experience that led him to compose most of the songs on his CD, *Dance with Me*:

> In a vision I saw a grand ballroom. Inside were guests – saints and angels – dressed in shining robes and white clothes. The guest of honor was Jesus. He was beautiful, dressed as a King, wearing the clothes of royalty. As I watched, He made His way down the staircase and onto the main dance floor. For several moments He stood there motionless, His eyes scanning the crowd. Soon whispers could be heard from the crowd. 'Dance… dance…' He simply shook His head.
>
> Slowly He turned towards the door. There He took off the beautiful adornments and crown and quickly stepped outside. It didn't take long for Him to find what He was looking for. I was there in the gutter, covered in dirt, looking terrible, smelling just as bad. He ran to me and smiled. 'Dance with me.'
>
> I just looked at Him. 'Jesus how can I possibly dance with You? Look at me! I could never come with You.' He spoke it again. 'Dance with me.' And with that he picked me up and began to carry me back to the ballroom, through the crowd, and up the staircase. We walked down the hallway and into another large room. Here there were no other guests. We danced alone as He began to sing.[1]

If I Could Only Believe in Love

Satan will do anything to try to separate us from the love of God. If we are unable to perceive God as infinitely loving toward us, we are unable to pursue Him with all our might – prayer becomes nothing more than absolute drudgery. This song describes the desire to believe in love:

> If I could only believe in love, like the first time
> If I could only see in Your eyes
> If I could only believe that this was the last time
> I would ever wonder
>
> I'd be dancing like a flame
> I'd be falling like the rain
> I'd be moving like the wind across the water
> I'd be dancing like a flame
> I'd be whispering Your name
> I will, if You'll let me be Your lover
> If You'll let me burn
>
> If I could only believe that time was the healer
> You know I would lift up my eyes
> If I could only believe my heart held the answers
> You could tear it wide again.[2]

God is love and He never changes. His love for us is not dependent on how well we are performing. It does not go up or down like a yoyo; it is always constant. He is not sitting up in heaven wanting to beat you over the head with a big stick. The Bible says that He loved us while we were yet sinners and that it is the kindness of God that leads us to repentance (Romans 2:4, 5:8).

In this chapter, I want to expose one of Satan's most effective strategies to separate us from God. I have called it 'The Great Deception'. I believe one thing keeps more people away from the secret place of communion than any other factor: condemnation.

The Subtle Power of Deception

The worst thing about deception is that when you are under its power you do not know that you are deceived. This has led many people to fear being deceived – and this fear itself is a deception. Ever since Adam and Eve sinned, the human race has been plagued with deceptive ideas about the nature and heart of God. The only way out of this is to place our faith in God's ability to lead us into truth, rather than be afraid of Satan's ability to deceive us.

The most effective deceptions are the subtlest ones. For example, when Satan tempted Eve to eat of the tree of the knowledge of good and evil, it seemed like a good thing to do. God had commanded that they should not eat of this particular tree but the way Satan described the fruit made it sound like a good thing to eat. He caused Eve to doubt the goodness of God.

The 'lust of the flesh', the 'lust of the eyes' and the 'pride of life' are all things that Satan uses to lure multitudes of people into deception (1 John 2:16). But let's assume you are aware of all these deceptions. You do not live primarily to satisfy the cravings of your flesh. You are not covetous with your eyes and you desire to walk in humility and dependence upon God. You may not be perfect at doing these three things but you are aware of them and continually seeking God to help you overcome. If Satan cannot keep us from God through these three things, his other primary strategy is to deceive us concerning God's love for us. Not only does he condemn and accuse us, he also accuses and questions the character and goodness of God. Jesus did not come to condemn but rather to save (deliver, restore, mend, heal, make whole). 'For God did not send His Son into the world to condemn the world, but that the world through Him might be saved' (John 3:17).

In Rick Joyner's book *The Final Quest*, he describes a vision in which multitudes of Christians were prisoners to the enemy primarily through the power of condemnation.

> Above the prisoners the sky was black with vultures named depression. Occasionally these would land on the shoulders of a prisoner and would vomit on him. The vomit was condemnation. When the vomit would hit a prisoner he would stand up and march a little straighter for a while, and then slump over even weaker than before…

As I watched, I realized that these prisoners thought that the vomit of Condemnation was truth from God… The only food provided for these prisoners was the vomit from the vultures. Those who refused to eat it simply weakened until they fell.³

Satan's strategy is so effective that multitudes believe that the condemnation that comes from Satan is actually truth from God. How then do we overcome this great bombardment that the enemy throws at us?

The Answer to Condemnation

The best way to overcome condemnation is to focus on what Jesus has done for us. He freely gave His life and took our punishment upon His body so that we could be righteous before God.

> But the free gift is not like the offense. For if by the one man's offense many died, much more the grace of God and the gift by the grace of the one Man, Jesus Christ, abounded to many. And the gift is not like that which came through the one who sinned. For the judgment which came from one offense resulted in condemnation, but the free gift which came from many offenses resulted in justification. For if by the one man's offense death reigned through the one, much more those who receive abundance of grace and of the gift of righteousness will reign in life through the One, Jesus Christ. Therefore, as through one man's offense judgment came to all men, resulting in condemnation, even so through one Man's righteous act the free gift came to all men, resulting in justification of life (Romans 5:15-18).

> He who believes in Him is not condemned; but he who does not believe is condemned already, because he has not believed in the name of the only begotten Son of God (John 3:18).

> There is no judgment awaiting those who trust him. But those who do not trust him have already been judged for not believing in the only Son of God (John 3:18, NLT).

We overcome condemnation by trusting in God's goodness toward us in Christ Jesus.

When we come into God's presence, Satan accuses and condemns us by saying, 'You are unworthy to come into the presence of a Holy God.' Our response should simply be, 'It is true that without Jesus I am completely unworthy to come into the presence of God, but because of Jesus' incredible gift of righteousness to me, I can come boldly and freely.' Does this mean that we are free to willfully sin? Absolutely not.

John 8:2-11 tells the story of a woman caught in the act of adultery. The scribes and Pharisees brought the woman to Jesus to trap Him. They knew that according to the law of Moses she should be stoned to death. They also knew that Jesus was merciful, so they anticipated that He would contradict the law of Moses. This would give them grounds to accuse Him of breaking the law. Rather than respond immediately, Jesus bided His time before saying, 'He who is without sin among you, let him throw a stone at her.' Everyone became so convicted by His words that they had to walk away. Only Jesus and the woman remained.

Jesus asked the woman two questions: 'Where are your accusers?' and 'Has no one condemned you?' Her response, 'No one, Lord,' shows that she had become convinced not only of her sin but also that Jesus was Lord. Jesus' response is beautiful: 'Neither do I condemn you; go and sin no more.' Jesus did not condemn this woman, but He did tell her not to sin anymore. Jesus' heart is to save us from our sins rather than destroy us in them.

It is important to understand the difference between wickedness and weakness. A wicked person is someone who habitually, deliberately and willfully sins against God. A weak person is someone who sincerely and wholeheartedly desires to overcome sin but who occasionally, and often even frequently, succumbs to sin because of the weakness of fallen humanity. God does not condemn us in our weakness. Like a child who stumbles and falls while walking toward daddy, God picks us up and encourages us to continue coming closer. This time we cling to His steadying hand even tighter.

Often we can be self-condemning because of past failure. Consider three examples from the Old Testament. Twice, out of fear for his life,

Abraham told his wife to lie about her identity and say that she was his sister, and yet the final summation of Abraham's life calls him the 'father of faith'. In the New Testament Job is held up as an example of patience and endurance and yet chapter after chapter in the book of Job is filled with his bitter complaining. David committed adultery in pursuing the heart of a married woman, and yet scripture records that he was a man after God's own heart. In all these examples repentance resulted in great weaknesses being turned into great strengths.

Do you find it hard to believe and trust in God's love for you? Has Satan deceived you about the goodness of God? Has he been working overtime to accuse and condemn both you and the character and nature of God? Perhaps he continually reminds you of events from the past that he orchestrated and now lies about, telling you it was God's fault. Does he tell you that God is not there for you or that compared to others you are not significant? All these things are part of Satan's great deception, making us feel isolated and distanced from God.

Our God loves us passionately. It is His desire for us to love Him passionately. The lies that Satan speaks about God's love and our worthiness to love God are passion killers that separate us from the heart of God. If you struggle with feeling betrayed by God, let me encourage you to seek some cross-centered counseling. The root issues involved can often be exposed and resolved in a few sessions. Restoring trust, however, takes time and requires a personal history of relating, whether it be with God or others.[4]

In Romans 8:31-39, Paul exposes Satan's lies about God's love for us by declaring the truth. Let me encourage you to meditate on these verses.

> What then shall we say to these things? If God is for us, who can be against us?
>
> He who did not spare His own Son, but delivered Him up for us all, how shall He not with Him also freely give us all things? Who shall bring a charge against God's elect? It is God who justifies. Who is he who condemns? It is Christ who died, and furthermore is also risen, who is even at the right hand of God, who also makes intercession for us. Who shall separate us from the love of Christ? Shall

tribulation, or distress, or persecution, or famine, or nakedness, or peril, or sword? As it is written: 'For Your sake we are killed all day long; We are accounted as sheep for the slaughter.' Yet in all these things we are more than conquerors through Him who loved us. For I am persuaded that neither death nor life, nor angels nor principalities nor powers, nor things present nor things to come, nor height nor depth, nor any other created thing, shall be able to separate us from the love of God which is in Christ Jesus our Lord (Romans 8:31-39).

Satan's lie is that God is against us, that we are condemned and have no hope. Paul declares that God is *for* us. Even in our weakness God's attitude toward us is one of benevolence and kindness. The ultimate evidence of God's love is the free gift of His Son, Jesus, who died on our behalf. Through this gift God has justified us – just as if we had never sinned. By refusing His free gift, we are saying that our sin is greater than His ability to justify us.

Satan's ministry is a ministry of condemnation and accusation. Jesus ministry is a ministry of intercession. Satan works overtime to try to separate us from the love of God. One of his primary ways of doing this is to use negative circumstances, past and present as evidence that God doesn't love us. Conquerors are made by focusing on God's great love in the midst of every circumstance.

> His love is higher
> Than the highest of mountains
> His love goes deeper
> Than the deepest of seas
> His love, it stretches
> To the farthest horizon
> And His love, it reaches to me
>
> His love is stronger
> Than the angels and demons
> His love, it keeps me

> In my life's darkest hour
> His love secures me
> On the pathway to heaven
> And His love is my strength and power
>
> His love is sweeter
> Than the sweetest of honey
> His love is better
> Than the choicest of wine
> His love, it satisfies
> The deepest of hunger
> And His love, in Jesus it's mine.[5]

Lord, your love is greater than we can fully understand. It is able to penetrate through every barrier or blockage in its path. Lord, help us to receive Your unconditional love in all circumstances.

Emotions: Expressed or Stifled

Another major barrier that keeps people from progressing in their relationship with God is an inability to be emotionally vulnerable. This was certainly true in my own life. I was often afraid when I was a child. Even at age 5, I was frightened that one day I would die. Although I had a father who loved me, he never really knew how to express this love and so I was very lonely. At the age of 12, I was so overwhelmed emotionally that I shut off my feelings in order to survive. I was a sensitive child and desperately needed to know emotional intimacy and love from my parents. All of these things became barriers to experiencing and knowing God better. Only after crying out to Him repeatedly was I able to break through these barriers and receive His touch.

When I first saw the Holy Spirit touching people, I became desperately hungry to receive the same thing. Like many others, however, I would lift my hands and wait but never experience the tangible reality of His presence. I cried out to God for six months before anything happened. I can still vividly remember the first time. I had attended a conference that went for two consecutive weeks, Thursday through Sunday. I spent the whole time desperately crying out for Him to touch me.

But at the end of the last meeting I was so disappointed that I gave up. I broke down and began to weep. Next thing, the warmth and love of God completely enveloped me. God promises that if we hunger and thirst after righteousness we *will* be filled (Matthew 5:6). Even though it took six months, I stayed hungry for God and didn't give up.

The first step towards being free from emotional-shutdown is to understand Jesus and His response to emotional intimacy.

Jesus and Emotion

God is a feeling God. Not only does He want us to share our hearts and feelings with Him, He also wants to share His heart and His feelings with us. Jesus was not afraid of emotional intimacy. This is demonstrated by the following event:

> Then one of the Pharisees asked Him to eat with him. And He went to the Pharisee's house, and sat down to eat. And behold, a woman in the city who was a sinner, when she knew that Jesus sat at the table in the Pharisee's house, brought an alabaster flask of fragrant oil, and stood at His feet behind Him weeping; and she began to wash His feet with her tears, and wiped them with the hair of her head; and she kissed His feet and anointed them with the fragrant oil. Now when the Pharisee who had invited Him saw this, he spoke to himself, saying, 'This man, if He were a prophet, would know who and what manner of woman this is who is touching Him, for she is a sinner.' And Jesus answered and said to him, 'Simon, I have something to say to you.' So he said, 'Teacher, say it.' 'There was a certain creditor who had two debtors. One owed five hundred denarii, and the other fifty. And when they had nothing with which to repay, he freely forgave them both. Tell Me, therefore, which of them will love him more?' Simon answered and said, 'I suppose the one whom he forgave more.' And He said to him, 'You have rightly judged.' Then He turned to the woman and said to Simon, 'Do you see this woman? I entered your

house; you gave Me no water for My feet, but she has washed My feet with her tears and wiped them with the hair of her head. You gave Me no kiss, but this woman has not ceased to kiss My feet since the time I came in. You did not anoint My head with oil, but this woman has anointed My feet with fragrant oil. Therefore I say to you, her sins, which are many, are forgiven, for she loved much. But to whom little is forgiven, the same loves little.' Then He said to her, 'Your sins are forgiven.' And those who sat at the table with Him began to say to themselves, 'Who is this who even forgives sins?' Then He said to the woman, 'Your faith has saved you. Go in peace' (Luke 7:36-50).

Consider the emotional intensity of this moment:

1. The words 'kissing' and 'anointing' in verse 38 are all in a continuous tense, meaning they happened not once but repeatedly.

2. This woman wept so much that she actually wet the feet of Jesus with her tears.

3. The word kissing implies not only a repeated action but is also an intensified word for kiss meaning to kiss earnestly.[1]

4. God's love had so touched this woman's heart that it caused her to anoint Him with costly fragrant oil.

Jesus did not rebuke her for any of these expressions of love. Most of us would feel uncomfortable with such a lavish expression of emotion and love, but Jesus was not. The emotion this woman felt was not something artificial or contrived. Let me make two further observations:

1. *Her emotion was based on divine revelation.* Firstly she was struck with grief that her sin caused her to wound the most loving heart in the universe. Secondly she was overwhelmed at His forgiveness despite the magnitude of her sin. Paul asked for revelation when he prayed, 'That the God of our Lord Jesus Christ, the Father of glory, may give to you

the spirit of wisdom and revelation in the knowledge of Him, the eyes of your understanding being enlightened' (Ephesians 1:17,18a). When we receive a greater experience and understanding of God, and the eyes of our heart are opened to see Him as He is, there is always an emotional response. The greater the revelation, the greater the emotional response.

2. *The emotion she felt moved her to action.* It caused her to prostrate herself at Jesus' feet as an expression of her gratitude. It is interesting that when we talk about someone being emotionally affected, we say they are 'moved'. Emotions have the power to move us to action. If an emotion causes us to draw closer to Jesus, it is, as the Amplified Bible calls it, a holy emotion (2 Corinthians 2:4 AMP).

This woman's story is not an isolated incident. There are many other examples of Jesus powerfully impacting people's lives. In fact John 21:25 says, 'And there are also many other things that Jesus did, which if they were written one by one, I suppose that even the world itself could not contain the books that would be written. Amen.'

Barriers to Emotional Intimacy

Jesus did not make the woman feel ashamed of her full expression of emotion, rather He affirmed her in her desire to abandon her old lifestyle and make Him the supreme obsession of her heart. Jesus longs for us to become vulnerable and transparent to Him.

Fear causes us to resist the experiential love of God. It causes us to resist the Holy Spirit, who pours love into our hearts. 'There is no fear in love; but perfect love casts out fear, because fear involves torment. But he who fears has not been made perfect in love' (1 John 4:18). The Holy Spirit is emotionally free. He is as unpredictable as the wind (John 3:8). One moment His mood can be tranquil and still, and then He shows Himself wild and untameable. In this sense the Holy Spirit is unpredictable but in the area of virtue He is totally predictable. He is always loving and kind, sometimes intense, at other times playful. The Holy Spirit has so much freedom that it sometimes frightens us. It is like free falling before the parachute cord is pulled. Here are some of the fears that stand in the way of trusting the Holy Spirit:

1. Fear of being out of control
2. Fear of emotion
3. Fear of being overwhelmed
4. Fear of intimacy
5. Fear of what others will think
6. Fear of letting go of something, or if we do let go of something, fear that He will not replace it with something better
7. Fear of exposure – after all, He is the Spirit of Truth
8. Fear of the unknown

These are fears God wants us, with His help, to overcome. I see two main ways people are prevented from experiencing the love of God:

1. Emotional intimacy has been a negative or abusive experience for a person.
2. Emotional intimacy is something a person has experienced very little of or not at all.

It can take time for those who have been subjected to abuse in the past to overcome their fear of emotional intimacy. This will affect their relationship with God. But God is gentle, caring and patient, and will not give us more than we can handle (1 Corinthians 10:13). He meets us where we are, and does not come to devastate and abuse, but rather to heal and restore.

If a person has not experienced emotional intimacy, particularly the loving touch of a father, he or she will most likely shy away from emotional intimacy. Many fathers do not know how to provide the nurture and love for their children that will develop trust and the ability to be truly intimate. To grow and develop as humans requires loving interaction with others, primarily our parents. God created our human spirit to function that way.

Without the foundation of loving interaction, trust can not be established. Without trusting relationships, a person has no place to process hurt, fear or pain. Consequently these things are pushed further from the surface. But to be emotionally intimate, a person has to feel the hurt and pain from the years of unaddressed and unresolved issues. God wants us to be able to bring these things to Him and let His perfect love cast out all fear. It is also important to allow others to be love with skin on.

Shame

Another major hindrance to being able to yield to the Holy Spirit is shame. Shame is the result of a person believing that he or she is defective and flawed. Guilt says, 'You have *done* something wrong.' Shame says, 'Who you *are* is wrong.' As a result of shame, we cover up who we really are so that others cannot see our defect or dysfunctions. Life becomes shallow if it is lived this way.

Emotions are an expression of who we are. For many, yielding to the Holy Spirit involves overcoming shamed emotions, for example, males might have been told, 'Boys don't cry' or 'Don't be a sissy'. Many people have grown up in homes where the free expression of grief or joy was frowned on. We should not be ruled or controlled by emotions, but part of our freedom in Christ is the freedom to be able to express the full depth of our sorrow or joy.

Shallow Emotion

Some will point out that we are called to live by faith – not by feelings. But there is a big difference between seeking to know God experientially and seeking to have an experience for its own sake. The difference is one of focus. The first is focused on knowing God, the second is focused on the experience itself. Those who passionately seek after God will experience Him but that experience will bring greater depth to the relationship. Those who seek experiences just for the purpose of having an experience become addicted to emotions. This results in a shallow relationship with

God and with others. Having only theoretical knowledge about God's love will do the same. The Bible says we love because we were first loved (1 John 4:19). We are unable to love without first experiencing the love of the Father. The degree to which we know His love is the degree to which we are able to love.

DRAWING NEAR TO GOD

In our pursuit of God we go through different stages. We know that God has made an open invitation for us to draw close to Him and that He does not place a limit on how close we can come. 'Draw near to God and He will draw near to you' (James 4:8). In drawing near to God, He calls us to three places – the barren place, the low place, and the high place.

The Barren Place

After God saved the Israelites and judged the Egyptians, who had held them captives for hundreds of years, He led His people out into the desert. He promised to give them a land flowing with milk and honey but first He led them into a wilderness. Why? The wilderness is a vitally important part of drawing near to God. It is a place of barrenness and solitude, a place where everything that is familiar and comfortable is taken away. We hate not having something to fill our lives up with – the wilderness seems so empty. We cry out to God, 'Give us anything but this' as we run around frantically trying to fill our lives, only to find at the end of the day that we are grasping at the wind.

If everything seems meaningless to you, then perhaps you are in the wilderness. On the surface there seems to be no progress, but God wants the roots of our lives to sink deeper into Him. For those who learn to embrace God's purpose, the wilderness is a surprisingly beautiful place.

> Therefore, behold, I will allure her,
> Will bring her into the wilderness,
> And speak comfort to her.

> I will give her her vineyards from there,
> And the Valley of Achor as a door of hope;
> She shall sing there,
> As in the days of her youth,
> As in the day when she came up from the land of Egypt
> (Hosea 2:14-15).

God is in the wilderness – not always in a dramatic sense – but He *is* there. He waits for us to become quiet and still enough to acknowledge His presence. The beauty of the wilderness is the beauty of being alone with God. It is here that a secret history is formed with God. It is here that we learn to live solely to please Him. Life here is lived in survival mode. Nothing more is required of us. God becomes our all in all. This place has done its work in your life when you can say, 'God, if you want me to die here, that's alright with me.'

The Low Place

When I was in my early teens, my father and mother, a family friend and I walked up a river valley and stayed the night in a small hut in the Southern Alps of New Zealand. I will never forget what it felt like to hike up this picturesque valley with mountains towering high above on both sides. A valley is a low place – a place that makes you realize how small *you* are, and how big *God* is (see Psalm 8).

Those who seek God's dwelling place, transform the low places that they pass through into places of refreshing.

> Blessed is the man whose strength is in You,
> Whose heart is set on pilgrimage.
> As they pass through the Valley of Baca (weeping),
> They make it a spring;
> The rain also covers it with pools.
> They go from strength to strength;
> Each one appears before God in Zion
> (Psalm 84:5-7, parenthesis added).

Even David acknowledged that in the valley of the shadow of death God's tangible presence was with him. 'Yea, though I walk through the valley of the shadow of death, I will fear no evil; for You are with me; Your rod and Your staff, they comfort me' (Psalm 23:4).

People worry about encountering resistance as they attempt to live their Christian lives. As we grow in Christ we become stronger and more able to withstand outside pressure. Human or demonic resistance is one thing, but it is much worse to have God Himself resist us. 'God resists the proud, but gives grace to the humble' (James 4:6), so as long as we have God on our side, no negative influence can overcome us.

The importance of humility is that it releases God's grace – His empowering presence. Pride tries to exist through self-sufficiency and independence. Humility stoops low in utter dependence on God. He is calling us to a low place, a place of humility.

> For thus says the High and Lofty One
> Who inhabits eternity, whose name is Holy:
> 'I dwell in the high and holy place,
> With him who has a contrite and humble spirit,
> To revive the spirit of the humble,
> And to revive the heart of the contrite ones' (Isaiah 57:15).

The doorway into God's kingdom is a low door. Humility is what allows us to pass through that door without extra baggage. 'Blessed are the poor in spirit, for theirs is the kingdom of heaven' (Matthew 5:3).

How low can you go? As sheaves of wheat ripen in the field, they bend over. The weeds (or 'tares' as the Bible calls them) on the other hand become more obvious because they stand up straight. 'The field is the world, the good seeds are the sons of the kingdom, but the tares are the sons of the wicked one' (Matthew 13:38).

For Jesus, our ultimate example, the cross was the lowest point in His journey:

> Let this mind be in you which was also in Christ Jesus, who, being in the form of God, did not consider it robbery to be equal with God,

but made Himself of no reputation, taking the form of a bondservant, and coming in the likeness of men.

And being found in appearance as a man, He humbled Himself and became obedient to the point of death, even the death of the cross. Therefore God also has highly exalted Him and given Him the name which is above every name, that at the name of Jesus every knee should bow, of those in heaven, and of those on earth, and of those under the earth, and that every tongue should confess that Jesus Christ is Lord, to the glory of God the Father (Philippians 2:5-11).

The High Place

As we have seen, God is calling us to a barren place and a low place, but He is also calling us to a high place. Moses spent forty years in the desert – a barren place. He then had an encounter with God that exposed his false humility and brought him to a low place – a place of complete dependence upon God. 'Now the man Moses was very humble, more than all men who were on the face of the earth' (Numbers 12:3). Then God called Moses up the mountain to meet with Him – the high place. Consider the following verses about high places:

> The Lord God is my strength; He will make my feet like deer's feet, and He will make me walk on my high hills (Habakkuk 3:19).

> If then you were raised with Christ, seek those things which are above, where Christ is, sitting at the right hand of God. Set your mind on things above, not on things on the earth. For you died, and your life is hidden with Christ in God. When Christ who is our life appears, then you also will appear with Him in glory (Colossians 3:1-4).

> For He has 'raised us up together, and made us sit together in the heavenly places in Christ Jesus' (Ephesians 2:6).

To draw near to God we need to have a desire for the high place, the place of spiritual vision and perspective. This is a place where we are free from earthly restraints and limitations, a place of unending glory where we touch the face and heart beat of God. God calls us to stand *in front of* His throne and promises that if we persevere we will sit with Him *on* His throne (Revelation 3:21). The throne of God is the highest place in the universe. It is reserved for those who are humble enough to seek God with all of their heart, soul, mind, and strength.

In the Song of Solomon, the Beloved (representing God) shows himself to the Shulamite maid (us).

> The voice of my beloved!
> Behold, he comes
> Leaping upon the mountains,
> Skipping upon the hills.
> My beloved is like a gazelle or a young stag.
> Behold, he stands behind our wall;
> He is looking through the windows,
> Gazing through the lattice (Song of Solomon 2:8-9).

The Shulamite maid is too frightened to step outside of her comfort zone to go with Him. He says she is like a frightened dove hiding in the clefts of the rock.

> O my dove, in the clefts of the rock,
> In the secret places of the cliff,
> Let me see your face,
> Let me hear your voice;
> For your voice is sweet,
> And your face is lovely (Song of Solomon 2:14).

As the Beloved continues to pursue the Shulamite maid, she gains the confidence and strength to venture out with Him. The song ends with the Shulamite beckoning to her beloved.

> Make haste, my beloved,
> And be like a gazelle

Or a young stag
On the mountains of spices (Song of Solomon 8:14).

God loves the kind of boldness, confidence and daring that beckons Him to venture out on the mountains. When God draws us to Himself He is inviting us to share the adventure of the high places. The Song of Solomon refers to these high places as 'mountains of spices'. They are mountains that exude the fragrance of passionate, enduring, adventurous and daring love.

THE ENCLOSED GARDEN: A STORY

The secret place is the place where passion begins. Condemnation, shame and fear have the power to keep us from this place but in Christ their power is destroyed. Now we can make the journey. Now we can begin the adventure. I have written this chapter as a story about one person's journey from fear and inadequacy to the beauty of bridal love. The obstacles this woman has to overcome and the lessons she learns are relevant to all of us. I pray that it will help you on your journey.

Awakened to Love

My heart beat faster with anticipation. For the first time in my life I felt like I had tasted true love. It had whetted my appetite for more. Now I couldn't be satisfied. I had to find out if it would last. I had to find out if it was real. But at the same time, I kept trying to quell the nagging fear that it was some cruel hoax. Never had I felt so insecure, so vulnerable, so unsure of myself.

I had searched for love all my life and each time the promises had vanished into thin air, increasing the agony in my heart and the desperation of my soul. But something propelled me to keep up my pursuit. I could think of nothing else that compared to the love I desired. Its origin was otherworldly, it came from somewhere beyond time and space, and yet so close, so near – it was eternal. It was infinite, unfailing. It came with a promise, but unlike the others, this one seemed real. I had been fooled before, but this was different. It was love so transparent and pure that there couldn't possibly be any darkness or deceit in it. The thought of the One who was the source of that love made me cry out to Him with every atom and fiber of my being. I could not stop myself. At one moment it felt like I was going to burst with rapturous love, at the next with intolerable pain.

'Oh, Lover of my soul, come and meet with me face to face, for your love is more delectable than all the finest delicacies of the earth and more exquisite than the finest work of an artisan.'

Apprehensive and unsure, I waited to see if He would answer me. What did He really think of me? I couldn't go on fooling myself. I had to know. Perhaps it was all a mistake. Why would a Lover so pure, so noble, and so kind want to have anything to do with me? Couldn't He see how plain and ordinary I was? Couldn't He see the lacerations and ugly scars I had received from those who were angry with me?

My inward focus and questioning mind caused my heart to sink in despair. I panicked. And suddenly I felt His gentle touch. It was my Lover. His touch began to quiet my anguished soul. I was so relieved that He was there, but I was also frightened that He would reject me, frightened that my cry to know true love would be forever unanswered.

'My Precious One, I will never turn My face away from you. Neither death nor life, angels nor principalities, things present nor things to come, nor any other created thing, shall separate you from My love.'

In my head I believed His words but my heart continually resisted His love. At times I would try to hide from Him, but He would always find me and patiently draw me out of my self-imposed isolation. Nothing would turn Him away. Slowly my heart began to embrace His love. His kindness began to strengthen and reassure me. I knew He was calling me to come and be with Him in His world – a world that was vastly different to anything I had known.

Rejecting Love's Invitation

His world had no limitations or boundaries. It was contrary to His nature to be limited. He was free. Too free. Free to love and free to be loved. I never knew such freedom existed, but I wanted it. It was irresistible, delightful and spontaneous. But it was also risky, and I knew it would cost me everything. His freedom frightened me, and yet I knew

He was calling me to join Him. My heart was like a walled city, locked and barred. I had tentatively let down some of my barriers to let Him in but He wanted all of me. Such exposure and vulnerability was too much. I could take it no longer. In desperation I pushed Him away.

'No my Lover! Go Your way and let me be at peace!'

I was shocked at what I had done. Confused and perplexed, I wandered about aimlessly, trying to reconcile the conflicting emotions in my heart. I was relieved and yet I ached. I wanted to push Him away and embrace Him all at the same time. Now I had done what I feared most, and become the one who created the divide between us. My own heart had betrayed what was most precious to me. The more time went on, the more intolerable I found the distance between us. I *had* to find Him. No matter what it took, I knew I had to find the One my soul loved. I simply could not live without Him.

> By night on my bed I sought the one I love; I sought him, but I did not find him. 'I will rise now,' I said, 'and go about the city; in the streets and in the squares I will seek the one I love.' I sought him, but I did not find him. The watchmen who go about the city found me; I said, 'Have you seen the one I love?' Scarcely had I passed by them, when I found the one I love. I held him and would not let him go, until I had brought him to the house of my mother, and into the chamber of her who conceived me (Song of Solomon 3:1-4).

Knowing the agitation of my soul, He quietly and gently affirmed me in His love. It was like cool streams of water washing over me. All I wanted was to be totally His, but I was fearful my heart would betray me once again.

'Lord help me to overcome my own weakness, fear and vulnerability. Teach me to hold my heart open to You even when it is painful. Cause my heart to run to You rather than away from You. Let me be Yours and Yours alone.'

His words of love and reassurance continued to wash me until I felt completely clean, completely safe, completely embraced. I relaxed my vice-like grip and melted into His embrace.

'Yes Lord, I choose to turn my back on what is familiar and safe. I want to be with You in Your world, I know that You will give me the strength to overcome.'

'My Precious one, if only you could know – you have ravished my heart with one look of your eyes.'

I was overwhelmed that my devotion to Him touched His heart so deeply. It was, after all, His devotion to me that now shone through my life. My heart was beginning to change. Whereas once I lived primarily for my own satisfaction and pleasure, now the desire of my heart was to bring satisfaction and pleasure to Him.

'Lord help me to be fully pleasing to You.'

The Garden

The atmosphere that surrounded me changed. The air was full of a most exquisite fragrance. I breathed in deeply and found to my surprise that we were in the midst of an enclosed garden. He looked at me to see what my reaction would be to the new surroundings. The picturesque garden was breathtakingly beautiful. Every direction I looked had enough beauty and color to make me want to stop and ponder for a lifetime. I looked back at Him filled with delight. He was pleased with my response.

'What you are feeling now is what I feel when I look at you.'

As hard as this was to fathom, I asked Him to help me try. He went on to explain that this garden personified my secret relationship with Him.

'When you turn your heart toward Me, even the slightest bit, this garden matures and sends out its fragrance for Me to enjoy.'

'Lord, let Your garden mature and send out its fragrance again and again.'

In answer to my request He took me to a spring in the middle of the garden. The water was fresh, cool and crystal clear. He invited me to sit on a small seat next to the spring. The seat was only big enough for the two of us. Sitting down beside me, He proceeded to tell me about the garden.

'Before time began, I dreamed of this place. Before the world existed

I envisioned it, I planned it meticulously. I smelt its pleasant fragrance, I dreamed of the time you would share it with Me. This garden is young and it is beautiful but what you see now is just the beginning of its full beauty. As you continue to let Me into the hidden places of your heart, this garden will grow. As you submit to My Lordship over your life in every circumstance and situation on the earth, this eternal garden matures. The connection between the eternal and the temporal is My Word and My Spirit. Both of these are eternal. I have given them to you. Treasure My Word. Let it penetrate into the depths of your heart and divide between soul and spirit. Treasure My Spirit, for it is He who will reveal to you things that no eye has seen, no ear has heard, things that have not entered into the heart of man. The Holy Spirit is a faithful steward of the mysteries hidden in Me. He searches all things, even the deep things of God. He will reveal to you the mystery of My love and prepare you to rule with Me as My Bride.'

As He looked into my eyes, the fire of His love burned deep into my soul.

'Yes Lord, I will be faithful to tend this garden.'

After He stood up and left I knelt down on my knees, closed my eyes and cried out with all my might.

'Awake O north wind, and come, O south!

Blow upon my garden, that its spices may flow out.

Let my beloved come to His garden and eat its pleasant fruits.'

The Book

I knew that to be fully pleasing to Him I would have to embrace not only the refreshing, warm summer wind but also the cold, bitter winter wind. But I was not alone. He had given me His Spirit and His Word.

As I opened my eyes I saw a book in front of me. It was His Word. I reached out and took hold of it. As I did I was connected with His heart. The book was living and active. I opened it and began to read. The words washed over me like cool, refreshing, cleansing waters – the summer wind.

The book was unlike any other I had ever read. The more I read the more it began to draw me into itself. It contained life-giving words that searched my heart. It was as if when I read, the book was reading me. The words went into my inmost being with piercing accuracy and cut away everything that was unlike Him. I had always tried to use His Word to achieve my own desires. This was the most searching and intense experience I had ever had. It was the winter wind. The core of my being was exposed as I saw more clearly how I had caused my Lover to be beaten, tormented and nailed to a tree.

I heard the voice of my Lover as I read. He was filled with holy jealousy for me to be completely His. The deeper the reality of the cross went into my heart, the more my self-centeredness cried out and screamed. I gripped the life-giving book until my knuckles turned white. As each thing was stripped away and dealt a deathblow, my love for Him increased, and I knew He would not be completely satisfied until the work was fully done. I had to choose to stay submitted to Him or distance myself from Him and His Word. Once I had been frightened of truth, now I was consumed with love for it.

The more I looked at Him the less I noticed my own weaknesses, fears and insecurities and the more I became like Him. My unworthiness was replaced by His kingly dignity, my shame was swallowed up in His glory, my fear was replaced by His forthrightness and courage as I learned to risk my inmost being with Him. The more His Word became part of me, the more I began to see myself as He saw me. Even in my weakness and frailty He saw me as His Bride, filled with dignity and honor.

The Ongoing Romance

Bridegroom:

O my love, you are as beautiful as Tirzah,
Lovely as Jerusalem,
Awesome as an army with banners!
Turn your eyes away from me,
For they have overcome me (Song of Solomon 6:4-5a).

Bride:

How can I overcome you, O mighty Prince?

Bridegroom:

You have overcome me by one glance of your eyes.

Bride:

My Lover, it is You who first overcame me with Your loving gaze.

Make haste, my beloved,
And be like a gazelle
Or a young stag
On the mountains of spices (Song of Solomon 8:14).

And our Bridegroom says:

To him who overcomes I will grant to sit with Me on My throne, as I also overcame and sat down with My Father on His throne (Revelation 3:21).

Part 4:

THE OUTWARD MISSION

THE FATHER'S DESIRE

Jesus' greatest passion and joy was to do the will of the Father. He only did what He saw His Father doing. If the Father was actively reaching the lost, Jesus was doing the same. Evangelism was His lifestyle. But He was not led by compulsion to witness to everyone. If the Father restrained Himself from reaching the lost, Jesus did likewise.

One of the promises that Jesus gave to His disciples was that He would give them His joy. God has designed evangelism to be a great joy rather than a great burden.

Today, forces are at work to hinder and abort evangelism. Mention the word 'evangelism' and a number of thoughts, pictures and associations immediately come to mind. For those who are gifted in that area, these scenes are often from past encounters with the unsaved. To them, evangelism is exciting, stimulating – perhaps at times disappointing – but most definitely a necessity of life. By far the larger group of Christians, however, are those who consider themselves ungifted in evangelism. For them, it is associated with feelings of guilt and condemnation.

It is not uncommon for a preacher to stand in front of a congregation, beating them with scriptures and using guilt to motivate them to reach the lost. The preacher is satisfied that he or she has preached well to lazy sluggards who don't care one iota if people go to hell, and the sad and sorry parishioners drag their feet out of the church, burdened with guilt but vowing to try better. Three of the most common scriptures used are:

1. He who wins souls is wise (Proverbs 11:30).

2. In Isaiah 6 the Lord says, 'Whom shall I send; and who will go for Us?' And Isaiah replies, 'Here am I! Send me.'

3. The great commission to go into all the world and make disciples as recorded in the gospels of Matthew, Mark and Luke.

Frequently these scriptures are taken out of the biblical context in which they occur. For example, Isaiah 6 is specifically about the call of God on Isaiah to proclaim God's message of judgment to the rebellious nation of Israel. And Proverbs 11:30 is not specifically about evangelism. When the Book of Proverbs was written, people were not classified as being saved or unsaved in the way that we think today. A wise person is able to 'win' a formerly offended, hostile, ignorant or disagreeable person, no matter what the issue. We must speak the message of the cross without compromise, and it is 'offensive' to our sin nature. But a wise person is sensitive and discerning, and will not offend *unnecessarily*. If we took hold of this wisdom in our everyday lives, including family, work and church relationships, we would be much better at evangelism. We will examine the great commission in more detail in chapter 11.

I do not believe that God wants us to be motivated by guilt into evangelism. Instead, I believe God wants to firebrand our hearts with *His* passion to save a lost and dying world.

My Journey

In my own journey of finding depth and intimacy with God, I started to realize how much He wanted me to be a witness for Him. I had a growing conviction in my life about reaching out to the lost. I say 'conviction' because it was not my personal desire. For much of my Christian walk I have felt completely passionless about reaching the lost. Rather than respond in guilt, I learned to be completely honest with God. 'God I do not feel any passion for the lost. This is not how I want to be, please give me more of Your heart.' Like most Christians I was terrified at the thought of witnessing to the unsaved, primarily because I feared embarrassment, humiliation, shame and rejection. I was particularly put off by evangelists who try to motivate people through guilt into witnessing. But the more I came to know God, the greater my conviction became, until finally I was able to step through my fear and begin talking to people.

During my time in Vanuatu with the children's ministry, Nelly, one of the children, had a vision of a long table with many crowns on it. Jesus told her that if they wanted souls they would have the crowns. 'Those who are wise shall shine like the brightness of the firmament, and those who turn many to righteousness like the stars forever and ever' (Daniel 12:3). Often as the children yielded to the Holy Spirit, a large crowd of additional children would be drawn. Some would participate, others would watch from a distance.

I will never forget one small boy who showed up one day. He was standing there with tears streaming down his face. Nobody knew who he was. Later he shared that he had had a vision of two roads. One was large and had many people on it. The other was narrow. All the children were on the narrow road and were rescuing those on the wide road.

God wants to give us all a vision like that. He also wants us to have childlike hearts that willingly receive *His* heart and *His* mission.

The Two Commandments

Jesus gives us two primary commandments to live by. The first is to love the Lord our God with all our heart, with all our soul, with all our mind, and with all our strength (Mark 12:30). The second is to love our neighbors as ourselves (Mark 12:31). It was my understanding that witnessing was part of the second commandment. Although this is true, God began to show me that witnessing is really an extension of the first commandment. Originally my thinking went something like this: I should love God first and then, once I have accomplished that with reasonable proficiency, I should think about the second commandment, which includes witnessing to the lost. However, the two commandments should not be considered as two separate and distinct entities. They are inseparable. In Luke's gospel the two are written as one statement. Both Matthew and Mark use the Greek word 'homoios', which means similar or alike, to show the unity of the two commands. The second command is the natural outworking of the first.

Why if these commands are inseparable did Jesus give two commands? The purpose of giving two commands is to help us see the priority and motivation we should have in obeying Him. Without having the first commandment as the priority in our lives, our love for others easily becomes either self-centered or a ritualistic and legalistic way of earning God's love. Our love for God is to be the motivation behind the second commandment, not an attempt to obtain God's love.

There are two misunderstandings that people have about these two commandments. Some let the second commandment become more important than the first. The result is a passionate evangelist with little true love and knowledge of God. Others think that you can obey the first commandment without obeying the second. The result is someone that pursues intimacy with God but lives in an enclosed world. God's love is so large it pours out of us. It is a river that flows constant and strong. It doesn't know seasons of drought and it never weakens or wavers. This love compels us to reach others just as we have been reached.

The Harvest

Jesus modeled the Father's heart to us by living among the lost. The Bible refers to the world as a harvest field.

Then Jesus went about all the cities and villages, teaching in their synagogues, preaching the gospel of the kingdom, and healing every sickness and every disease among the people. But when He saw the multitudes, He was moved with compassion for them, because they were weary and scattered, like sheep having no shepherd. Then He said to His disciples, 'The harvest truly is plentiful, but the laborers are few. Therefore pray the Lord of the harvest to send out laborers into His harvest' (Matthew 9:35-38).

As He walked among the crowds of people who needed His help, He was moved with compassion. So often we want it to work the other way around, to be moved and then to act. Jesus makes it clear that it is God's harvest field. This teaches us two things. Firstly, that God takes ownership of the harvest field. This releases a great weight from us. It is not our harvest field but His. Secondly, it teaches us to serve. We are not doing a work and asking God to help us. It is His harvest field and by working in it we are serving Him. The harvest is the Father's business. He owns it, He operates it and He intends it to be fruitful. As sons and daughters of God we are to take ownership of the task with Him.

The Way of the Master

A few years ago, God led me to start a church and gave me three clear mandates. As a church we were to advance in the supernatural, in business and finance, and in evangelism. The only problem was that the people in the church took great interest in supernatural and prophetic ministry and were not at all interested in evangelism. In fact many of them were adamantly against it. I have never considered myself an 'evangelist', but as the leader of a church I knew that I was responsible to help lay the foundations that were weak or non-existent. In my attempt to do this, I discovered a course called *The Way of the Master* by Ray Comfort and Kirk Cameron.[1] The course consisted of eight half-hour DVDs that had been produced for television. This course revolutionized my understanding of evangelism. From a theological perspective, it showed how modern evangelism has abandoned the use of the law, particularly the Ten Commandments, to bring the conviction of sin. This has made much of our witnessing powerless and ineffective. I began to see how foundational this truth was to New Testament teaching. John the Baptist, Jesus, Peter, Stephen, Paul, James and Jude all used the law to bring the conviction of sin in order to lead sinners to the cross.

The other thing that impressed me about *The Way of the Master* was how practical the teaching was. Each DVD had real life footage of street witnessing that made you feel like you were there. It made the whole process so simple that anybody could learn how to witness effectively and powerfully. For most people, the idea of going out to witness is like being on a battlefield without weapons. But by using *The Way of the Master* I found that people were often happy and willing to talk. I didn't need to have the answers to everyone's intellectual or argumentative questions because it had taught me to appeal to the conscience rather than the intellect. God has given everyone a conscience that witnesses to God's law (Romans 2:15). Even when the conscience is seared, the knife of the law and the conviction of the Holy Spirit are able to penetrate the heart. I also found that my dignity and the dignity of the people I was witnessing to were left intact. There was no haranguing or 'holier than thou' attitude – just polite, enjoyable and earnest conversation. Rather than trying to win a person around to my point of view I was simply able to express my concern at the possibility of them spending an eternity in hell. If a person was hardened towards the message I could continue to use the law to bring the conviction of sin, but if they were open I could bring them the message of grace for salvation.

The first six times I went out on the streets were not easy. But I was overcoming my fear of what people thought of me. In that battle against fear, it was helpful to remember that the worst thing that could happen to me was rejection. The worst thing that could happen to them was that they would spend eternity in hell. As I meditated on this truth, compassion swallowed my fears.

After overcoming my fear I became more and more proficient in using the simple but powerful tools I had been equipped with. I found that my confidence helped to put people at ease. I learned from my mistakes, and became better at saying the right things at the right time.

After going out on the streets once a week or once a fortnight over a period of months, I began to see people as lost souls who needed God. I had started out ill-equipped and afraid, but now I was able to go out on the streets for an hour or more and sometimes speak to over ten people. By faithfully doing this, I began to enjoy the task. It has connected me with my city in a very tangible way.

Individual Gifting Versus Corporate Mandate

The Charismatic and Prophetic movements have tended to emphasize the idea that people have specific gifts. For example, some people are Intercessors while others are Evangelists. This often results in a scenario where Intercessors do the praying and Evangelists do the witnessing. If an Evangelist doesn't like prayer and an Intercessor doesn't like evangelism they can come to a simple agreement: let the Evangelist evangelize while the Intercessor prays. But I believe this leads to less effectiveness. If Evangelists make prayer a regular part of their lives, their evangelism becomes more effective. Likewise, if Intercessors make evangelism a regular part of their lives, they become better Intercessors. Scripture exhorts all believers to be fully equipped to advance God's Kingdom on earth. Part of that equipping, among other things, is prayer and witnessing. Without these foundations we are ill equipped. God has not left us without help for the task of being His witnesses. Firstly, He has given us the Holy Spirit. Secondly, He has given us the ministries of apostle, prophet, evangelist, pastor and teacher to equip and train us. These five ministries have been given as gifts to the Body of Christ. One of the most important aspects of intimacy with God is learning to receive the gifts that He gives us. In order to be fully equipped for the task, I believe we have to submit to all five ministries. Unfortunately many Christians are selective in what they will receive from God. It is like God gives us five beautiful gold rings. We take two or three of them and throw the others away. This grieves the heart of God because all the gifts are equally important and freely given.

Jesus and Soul-Winning

The greatest soul-winner of all was Jesus Himself. His life teaches us a great deal about the noble art of soul-winning. John chapter 4 tells the story of Jesus' encounter with a Samaritan women. He and His disciples were traveling from Judea in southern Israel to Galilee in the north. To do this they had to pass through the territory of Samaria. The Samaritans had broken away from Israel hundreds of years earlier and had formed their own version of Judaism. They were despised by the Israelites. Jesus and His disciples arrived in Samaria weary from their journey and in need of food and refreshment. The disciples went into a nearby town called Sychar to get food, and Jesus waited outside the town at the local well.

While the disciples were away, a Samaritan woman came out from the town to draw water at the well. Jesus began speaking to her and during their conversation, Jesus revealed by a word of knowledge that He knew that the woman had had five husbands and that the man she was presently with was not her husband. When you realize that somebody knows the details of your life, including your thoughts, actions, motives and history, it brings great conviction, particularly when that somebody is God. Such knowledge creates a sharpened awareness of the responsibility we carry for everything we think, say or do. The events and conversations that followed reveal many things about Jesus' perspective on evangelism.

> And at this point His disciples came, and they marveled that He talked with a woman; yet no one said, 'What do You seek?' or, 'Why are You talking with her?' (John 4:27)

It is important to note that Jesus was often found in the harvest field. Although Jesus taught in synagogues – the churches of the day – He also spent time in the marketplace, interacting with people as they went about their daily lives. This incident happened at a well, which was a common gathering place. However, it was not normal for someone to get water during the heat of the day. Jesus recognized a divine appointment in the midst of circumstances that were a little unusual. He also crossed cultural boundaries by talking to a Samaritan and by talking to a woman. This woman became the key that brought salvation to many in the town of Sychar.

The woman then left her waterpot, went her way into the city, and said to the men, 'Come, see a Man who told me all things that I ever did. Could this be the Christ?' Then they went out of the city and came to Him. In the meantime His disciples urged Him, saying, 'Rabbi, eat.' But He said to them, 'I have food to eat of which you do not know.' Therefore the disciples said to one another, 'Has anyone brought Him anything to eat?' Jesus said to them, 'My food is to do the will of Him who sent Me, and to finish His work' (John 4:28-34).

Jesus' statement, 'My food is to do the will of Him who sent me, and to finish His work', is loaded with meaning. It is clear that for Jesus the work of evangelism was both enjoyable and necessary – just as food is. Rather than being a burden, the work of evangelism energized, sustained and refreshed Jesus. God intends the same for us. Jesus' statement contains two profound but simple revelations. Firstly, harvesting is the Father's will, and secondly, the harvest is the Father's work. The harvest is the Father's fervent desire. As we come to know and love the Father, His desire and work become ours. The key that unlocks the harvest is the Father's love. If we could fully grasp this truth, the work of evangelism would become as enjoyable and necessary to us as our daily food.

> Do you not say, 'There are still four months and then comes the harvest'? Behold, I say to you, lift up your eyes and look at the fields, for they are already white for harvest! (John 4:35)

The disciples were inclined to think of the harvest as being something in the future. However, Jesus clearly exhorted them not to speak of a future harvest but to bring it into the present. Why is this important? It is imperative to understand that not only is harvesting the Father's will and work, but it is also His present occupation. The reason the disciples were unaware of the present harvest was because they were only seeing the situation with limited natural perception. When Jesus said, 'Lift up your eyes', He was saying, 'Look where you are not presently looking'. He told them to look more closely and keenly at the harvest field that was all around them. The Greek word for 'look' means to look closely at, to perceive – an earnest and prolonged inspection with careful contemplation.

It is hard to capture the emotion behind Jesus' words by reading our English translations. The Greek makes it clear that Jesus was demonstrative about His Father's harvest field. '*Behold*, I say to you, *lift up your eyes* and *look* at the fields, for they are already white for harvest!' In the Greek this sentence has three imperatives in it. I have shown this by putting them in italics. One imperative in a sentence makes the statement strong but three imperatives in one sentence shows very strong language. The first imperative is the word 'behold'. The Greek word used is defined in grammatical terms as a demonstrative participle. Demonstrative means given to or marked by the open expression of emotion. More than just a word, it is like an emotional gasp. That is why

Passion and Fire

I like the King James Bible, which translates the word as 'Lo!'

> And he who reaps receives wages, and gathers fruit for eternal life, that both he who sows and he who reaps may rejoice together. For in this the saying is true: 'One sows and another reaps.' I sent you to reap that for which you have not labored; others have labored, and you have entered into their labors (John 4:36-38).

There are two great blessings that are given to those who participate in God's harvest field. The first is reaping salvation where other people have begun the work of sowing truth into a person's heart. The second is sowing truth into people's lives so that others can be used in reaping salvation. The disciples and Jesus could reap because of the work that John the Baptist and his disciples had already done. John the Baptist began his ministry just six months earlier than Jesus. There is not necessarily a long time between sowing and reaping, and Jesus says that both the sower and the reaper are able to rejoice together. The word 'together' means at the same time and place. The disciples were about to be used to help reap a harvest that Jesus had begun by sowing truth into the Samaritan woman's life.

What follows in this story is truly remarkable – the Samaritan woman became instrumental in bringing many to Jesus. The people of the town urged Jesus to stay with them. They came to believe, not because of what the woman said to them, but because they had heard Jesus for themselves. True evangelism brings a person into a living, dynamic encounter with God Himself. We must not stop short of this. *Our* witness is to bring people to Jesus. In the past a lot of effort has gone into bringing people to a particular church or personality. So often the aim has been to bring people to our way of thinking or believing. Instead, we should strive to lead people into a personal encounter with Jesus, not only as Savior but also as Lord.

The encounter between Jesus and the Samaritan woman illustrates five significant truths for today's harvest field:

1. God knows every person in our towns and cities

2. He knows the ones who are ripe for salvation
3. He knows the ones who are strategic to bring salvation to many
4. He knows how to connect us with them
5. He knows the strategies that will reach them

INTERCEPTING OUR GENERATION

Jesus' entire ministry was based on impacting the lives of everyday people. He intercepted His generation by offering them a completely new way of living. The result was that many were turned from darkness to light. How did He do this? What sort of a person was Jesus? The Bible tells us that He spent the majority of His life as a businessman, a carpenter, 'growing in favor and stature with God and with men'. The passion and intensity of His love for God would be hard to calculate in human terms, but it is also important to recognize that Jesus loved and was concerned about *people*. During His three and a half years of public ministry, He immersed himself in the harvest field but also took time to get away from the crowd to be with His Father. He called His disciples to follow this example.

Seeking and Saving the Lost

There was something about Jesus that made Him attractive to sinners. In His presence they felt accepted and loved. 'Then all the tax collectors and the sinners drew near to Him to hear Him. And the Pharisees and scribes complained, saying, "This Man receives sinners and eats with them"' (Luke 15:1-2).

Jesus attracted sinners! It was the devoutly religious who were repelled and offended by Him. I suspect that if we had been alive when Jesus walked the earth, we would have been offended by Him at times as well. Self-righteousness is subtle. It creeps in by stealth and blinds its victim. To such people Jesus spoke three parables:

What man of you, having a hundred sheep, if he loses one of them,

> does not leave the ninety-nine in the wilderness, and go after the one which is lost until he finds it? And when he has found it, he lays it on his shoulders, rejoicing. And when he comes home, he calls together his friends and neighbors, saying to them, 'Rejoice with me, for I have found my sheep which was lost!' I say to you that likewise there will be more joy in heaven over one sinner who repents than over ninety-nine just persons who need no repentance (Luke 15:4-7).

Middle Eastern shepherds knew every one of their sheep by name, and could tell if any were missing. Jesus appears to be making a subtle, or perhaps not so subtle, reference to Ezekiel 34 in which Israel's shepherds (leaders) were condemned for only being concerned about their own comfort and not seeking the lost. For the Pharisees and scribes, who were familiar with the Scriptures, this would have been a strong rebuke.

> Or what woman, having ten silver coins, if she loses one coin, does not light a lamp, sweep the house, and search carefully until she finds it? And when she has found it, she calls her friends and neighbors together, saying, 'Rejoice with me, for I have found the piece which I lost!' Likewise, I say to you, there is joy in the presence of the angels of God over one sinner who repents (Luke 15:8-10).

The footnote in the New King James Version says that valuable coins were often worn in a ten-piece garland by married women. The garland was precious because it was a covenant gift from the woman's husband. It spoke of the intimacy between them. In the same way, God had a special covenant with the nation of Israel, and to Him the Israelites who had strayed away from Him were as precious as the lost coin was to the woman in the story (Ezekiel 16:8,10-14).

Finally, Jesus drove His point home with a third parable about two sons (Luke 15:11-32). The younger son demanded his share of the inheritance from his father and then promptly left home and wasted what he had been given on riotous living. After all his money was gone he kept himself alive by taking a job feeding pigs and sharing their food. Finally he returned to his father, pleading to be accepted as a slave. The father, who had been heartbroken over his son's departure welcomed him back like royalty and celebrated with a huge feast. The son was restored but his older brother, who had always been faithful to his father, was jealous and angry about all the attention the younger son was receiving.

This parable is usually known as 'The Parable of the Prodigal Son'. But there are really two prodigal sons in the story. The younger son represents sinners and those who have turned their backs on a covenant relationship with God. The older son represents the Pharisees and scribes who stayed with the Father but did not have a close relationship with Him because of the attitudes of their hearts. Jesus welcomed the sinners who were being drawn back into a covenant relationship with Him and paid the cost of offending those who were like the older brother.

These three parables speak of close and intimate relationships: that of a shepherd to his sheep, a woman to her husband, and a father to his sons. In each parable something valuable is lost and the person goes seeking, until with great joy, they receive back what has been lost.

In the church, our message has often catered for the peace and the security of the ninety-nine that are already in the sheepfold. But God's heart is always urging us to pursue those who have strayed and lost their way. God sees the people of all the nations of the earth as His 'inheritance'. They are of greater value and worth to Him than any other created thing. In Psalm 2:8 David speaks prophetically, showing us God the Father's exhortation to the Messiah King, Jesus. 'Ask of Me, and I will give You the nations for Your inheritance, and the ends of the earth for Your possession.' We are each part of the answer to Jesus' prayer. He asks us to join with Him in obtaining His inheritance. Through His death, the nations were purchased for God. We are privileged to be able to help bring in the reward of this sacrifice.

There are four ways that Jesus intercepted His generation, and His methods are the benchmark for today's disciples:

1. *Jesus intercepted people in the course of everyday life (John 4).* Even though He was hungry, tired and thirsty, Jesus recognized a strategic God-ordained opportunity when the Samaritan woman arrived at the well. How many times do we miss these encounters in our own lives

because we have become so caught up in the hustle and bustle of 21st century living? The women came to the well to fetch water almost every day – it was a regular chore. The only reason this particular day was different was that Jesus' spirit was open to her. Jesus Himself was only at the well because of some unfavorable circumstances in His own life. This encounter happened as Jesus was moving from Judea in the south of Israel to Galilee in the north. Samaria was the region between Judah and Galilee. The reason that Jesus left Judea was because His disciples were baptizing more people than John the Baptist. This was creating conflict with the Pharisees. Not wanting to stir up strife Jesus moved from the area. This encounter at the well may not have happened were it not for the unfavorable circumstances in Judea.

2. Jesus deliberately and intentionally went to the harvest field. As we have already seen, Jesus was deliberate and intentional about immersing Himself in His Father's harvest field (Matthew 9:35).

3. Jesus was led by the Spirit. Although there are many instances of Jesus being specifically led by the Spirit of God, I will use the example of a man called Simeon found in Luke 2:25-35. Simeon had received a promise from the Holy Spirit that he would not die until he had seen Jesus. On the day that Mary and Joseph brought Jesus to the temple for dedication, the Spirit prompted Simeon to go there. Simeon saw the child Jesus and blessed him, then prophesied that Jesus would bring light to the Gentiles. He was saying in effect that Jesus would intercept His generation not only in Israel but also in other nations. Just as Simeon was specifically led to the temple by the Spirit, we will also be led to bring the message of salvation in specific situations. Just as Simeon saw Jesus' destiny even though Jesus was only an infant, we need to have the ability to see the destiny that is lying dormant in unbelievers – they are the apostles, prophets, evangelists, pastors and teachers of tomorrow.

4. Jesus was 'enquired of' (Luke 18:18-24). It would be great if everybody just walked up to us and started asking about Christianity, rather than us needing to talk to them. If we examine the story of the rich young ruler in Luke 18, it is clear that the young man was able to speak to Jesus because Jesus was accessible. He was out and about where people could see Him and ask Him questions. Jesus knew that the man's riches were an idol to him and told him to sell everything. The ruler didn't like what Jesus said and went away sad. Jesus was also grieved at this response. The work of evangelism can be both exhilarating and troubling. It is exhilarating when people turn from darkness to light. It is troubling when people are not prepared to face their sin, and deliberately walk away from salvation. But no matter what the response, the greatest fulfillment and exhilaration for the evangelist comes from doing the Father's will and working alongside Him as He engages in His work.

Another man who intercepted his generation effectively was Philip. The ways he did this are recorded in Acts, and are very similar to the methods we have just discussed:

1. *A change in circumstance.* The church in Jerusalem was used dramatically by God as a witness in their own city. Philip was one of the seven who were chosen to be deacons of this group and had faithfully served in that capacity. However, after a time a great persecution arose and the believers were scattered throughout Judea and Samaria (Acts 8:1). For Philip this resulted in a dramatic change of circumstance that would also, as we shall see, bring many new people to salvation. The persecution was something that he had no power over but it did not stop him from being a faithful witness. He was going about his everyday life in the midst of unfavorable circumstances and found opportunity to bring in a great harvest of souls.

2. *He went to them.* When the persecution arose, Philip went to Samaria and preached Christ to them (Acts 8:5). This was a deliberate action. His preaching and the miracles that he performed had such power that the entire city was impacted. What appeared to be a negative change in circumstances had turned out to be an incredible opportunity to bring salvation and deliverance to the city of Samaria.

3. *Directed by the Spirit.* After a time Philip had an encounter with an angel (Acts 8:26). The angel instructed him to go south into a desert region where there would be few people. In obedience he left the masses in Samaria and journeyed south until he met an Ethiopian official riding in a chariot and reading from the book of Isaiah. The Spirit of God told Philip to draw near and overtake the chariot. Philip did so and asked the man if he understood what he was reading.

4. *He was enquired of.* The Ethiopian man replied, 'How can I, unless someone guides me?' This was the first of three questions the man asked Philip. His second enquiry to Philip was, 'Of whom does the prophet say this, of himself or of some other man?' (Acts 8:34). The third enquiry was, 'What hinders me from being baptized?' (Acts 8:36). Philip was able to explain the prophecy to the man, lead him to salvation and finally baptize him in some water close to the road. At God's leading Philip left the masses in Samaria to witness to one man. In turn, that man had great authority and influence in his own nation.

5. *Snatched away by the Spirit.* After Philip had baptized the Ethiopian, the Spirit snatched Philip away supernaturally and took him to a town called Azotus, on the southern coast of Israel. Philip preached in all the cities along his path until he came to Caesarea, on the northern coast of Israel. In this way Philip was used to bring salvation to the entire coastal region of Israel.

Philip began as a faithful witness in his hometown. When the persecution broke out he went to Samaria where God used him to shake an entire city. Then he was directed by the Spirit to witness to a man with influence over an entire nation. The instant he had done this he was snatched away by the Spirit and used to bring salvation to the entire coastal region of Israel.

Jesus and Philip intercepted their generations. Their all-consuming love for the Father ignited a fiery passion to reach the lost. Their lives leave a clear message to us today. The message is simple – let the Father's love so consume you that you become a fiery witness for Him. Welcome and embrace every one of the different ways that God used Jesus and Philip. Respond to every opportunity that God gives so that He can open doors of opportunity on a level you never imagined possible.

The Two Most Powerful Weapons

In talking with people on the street, I have often noticed that even when they are not convicted by the truth about sin and its consequences they are moved when I tell them that I am speaking to them because I don't want anyone to go to hell. Concern for people's eternal well-being communicates love to them. Love has the power to disarm people who are resistant to truth.

Truth by itself exposes the heart, but love has the power to win the heart over to truth. When love is our motivation it gives us a unique advantage in the battle for the lost. Love enables us to see into people's hearts. It gives us true discernment. Paul made this clear when he prayed that the Philippians' love would abound more and more in knowledge and discernment (Philippians 1:9). Jesus saw into the Samaritan woman's heart. She was desperate for truth, even though that truth was painful. When the secrets of her heart were exposed, she in turn became a great evangelist and many in her city believed. Jesus did not reveal who He was straight away but drew her out of herself so that she could make that discovery. Truth is a weapon that we must use, but not in a way that short-circuits or blocks a person's process of discovery.

Jesus does not see people as objects nor view them as statistics in the 'saved' or 'unsaved' column. What He saw in the Samaritan woman was an earnest heart in search of truth. She was captured by the fact that Jesus could see deep into her heart. When she said, 'He told me everything I ever did', she was saying that He had exposed the foundational motivations that were behind everything she ever did.

This is what Paul meant when he said in 1 Corinthians 14:24-25, 'But if all prophesy, and an unbeliever or an uninformed person comes in, he is convinced by all, he is convicted by all. And thus the secrets of his heart are revealed; and so, falling down on his face, he will worship God and report that God is truly among you' (1 Corinthians 14:24-25).

In order to evangelize effectively, we need to pray continually, 'Lord, help me to see people as You see them.' Ultimately, passion for God leads to compassion for people. As the evangelist Trevor Yaxley says, 'A vision that thrusts a man's encapsulated heart out into the unfathomable realms of human depravity and causes an immediate active response is truly a vision of profound significance. Only the Father's heart knows the depth of love that emanates from such a life.'

Jesus' conversation with the Samaritan woman could be summed up under two headings – water (which spoke of desire) and worship. Jesus offered to give her water that would cause her never to thirst again. The woman could easily relate to the conversation.

If Jesus were talking to a heartsick teenage girl in our day, He might well talk to her about a clothing outlet that gives away clothes that never fade or go out of fashion. For a young girl desperate to be beautiful, this would be a dream come true. After all, the desire to be beautiful is a legitimate God-given desire, it is the enemy who has perverted it. She would certainly be curious about Him saying such an odd thing. After Jesus had revealed His true identity, she might say that the pop 'goddesses' that her culture worships encourage her to flaunt her body and be morally free (immoral), whereas the Christians down the road worship differently. It doesn't seem as interesting or as freeing as her lifestyle. Just to test Him out she might go on to say that she was saved in an evangelistic meeting when she was a little girl; surely she can worship God and her pop stars, after all, they always talk about love (consensual sex), beauty, peace and other good things.

But in her heart she is sick and tired of striving to be attractive to win the approval and acceptance of those around her.

Jesus might respond by saying that those who are truly beautiful are those who worship God and reflect His beauty. This would create a contrast between the beauty and love she had obtained through her own strength, and God's beauty and love – which is infinitely better. His offer to give her His love when she knew she didn't deserve it would be such a great kindness that it would bring her to repentance.

Overcome with gratefulness that Jesus had loved her enough to tell her the truth, she would now have a taste of being truly loved and truly beautiful for the first time in her life. She would go and tell her friends that she had met a man who knew the depths of her heart, could deal with the waywardness of sin and answer the deepest desires of her heart.

Jesus used language that exposed and captured the heart. He did this by using the powerful weapon of truth coupled with the even more powerful weapon of love.

The Invitation

I wrote the following story as a way of encouraging us all to become fishers of men.

Naphtali lay awake. Sleep seemed far from him tonight. He could hear the sound of his parents, brothers and sisters breathing steadily, tired from the arduous journey they had made over the last two days. Naphtali was used to making regular treks down to Jerusalem with the family to observe religious ceremonies and feasts. These occasions were filled with the excitement of going to the big city with all its activity, color and diversity. All the teachings of the Rabbis seemed more real in Jerusalem. Somehow the things he was taught at synagogue had a new dimension of meaning. The temple and sacrifices were there right before his eyes.

Although Naphtali often looked forward to such expeditions, tonight was different. His mind was occupied with an altogether different scenario. He and his family, along with multitudes of others, had been out in the barren countryside that surrounded the Sea of Galilee. This had nothing to do with any religious ceremony; this was to do with a man named Jesus. He was so ordinary and yet so different. Something about this man captured your heart. Naphtali thought about how they had sat all day in the hot Judean sun listening to this man teach. They had hardly noticed the uncomfortable conditions as they were captivated by the man's words. There were thousands of people there, and no one wanted to leave.

Capernaum, where Naphtali lived, was a fisherman's town. Nothing great – although he liked living by the water. No famous prophets had come from here and nothing of much significance had ever occurred.

He enjoyed going with the other boys to the synagogue each day and learning about the Torah, the Word of God. He had memorized much of it already. Zechariah, his teacher, taught with enthusiasm, taking personal interest in each boy. Napthali also loved going fishing with his father. He had learned a lot from his parents. Their integrity and dedication to God spoke for itself. He was struck by the stories they told of the great men of faith, like Moses, Samson and Elijah, and the coming Messiah.

As Naphtali lay there thinking, his mind went back to the events of the last eighteen months. When Jesus arrived, no one was unaffected. There were healings and miracles – Peter's mother-in-law, the man with leprosy, the paralytic, the man with the withered hand. Jairus' daughter had been raised from the dead. As long as Jesus was in town, there was a continual string of miracles and a continual crowd of people.

There was nowhere on earth Naphtali wanted to live more than in Capernaum, and he was awed by the fact that Jesus kept coming back. People would often come to town seeking Jesus. Naphtali's parents had opened their home to frequent guests. But Jesus had also created divisions. Relationships were strained between those who embraced Jesus and those who didn't – often between members of the same family.

Yesterday, something incredible had happened. The crowd had been listening to Jesus all day and no-one had eaten. Late in the day, the disciples organized everyone into groups of about one hundred. Naphtali saw Jesus praying over a boy's lunch, and next thing, the disciples started handing out food to everyone – from nowhere! People were so shocked that an audible wave of exclamation flowed across the crowd. The disciples looked stunned, then puzzled, then overjoyed. They kept looking back at Jesus with amazement.

Naphtali's heart raced as he thought about what had happened. Everybody else saw an awesome miracle and a free meal, but Naphtali couldn't help looking beyond the bread and fish to Jesus. Jesus' eyes had so much compassion in them – they seemed to speak a language that Naphtali didn't fully understand. Jesus' eyes seemed to tell Naphtali that he could never be truly satisfied by following in his father's footsteps catching fish. Jesus was calling him to be a fisher of men. The more he thought about the look in Jesus' eyes the more he could sense the infinite worth that God placed on every person.

Naphtali rolled over and tried to sleep, but he knew that he would have no rest until he answered Jesus' invitation.

IGNITING PASSION FOR THE LOST

The question is, how do we ignite our passion for the lost? Sometimes that desire is hard to find, but even if our hearts are dry there is hope. When dry tinder ignites, it burns hot and fierce. The flame of God's love turns apathy into action, fear into faith, barrenness into fruitfulness and callousness into courageous zeal.

The first step is being honest about the condition of our hearts. The following is a vision received by a man named Dave Anthes:

> I saw a large rock surrounded on all sides by waves of water splashing against it. No matter how hard they splashed, the rock did not move. I then saw that there were people on the rock and the rock started to grow bigger, but the waves also grew larger. I could also see that the people were involved in different activities.
>
> Some were feasting at tables. The food was just lying out for anyone to eat, and it was free and available to everyone. Others were playing games and seemed oblivious to the other people around them. Few of these people even seemed to know that they were on a rock. Others were sleeping, and seemed very comfortable.
>
> Other people were standing close to the edge, helping others to climb out of the sea. Still others were climbing the sheer face of the rock, trying to get on top. At times, the waves of the sea would crash against these people and wash them back into the ocean. Some would swim back and start to climb again, but others were lost.
>
> As the vision 'pulled away', I saw the name 'Jesus' written on the rock. What stood out to me was that most of the people were staying in the middle, having a lot of fun for themselves, and seemed

unaware of the tragedy going on around them. The only ones who were helping others were those on the edge.[1]

Where do you fit in this vision? Are you sleeping, playing games or feasting on the rock? Or are you one of those helping others out of the sea? Maybe you have become aware of the treacherous ocean and its victims but are frightened to help or simply don't know how. Whatever the case, here are four important keys that can help ignite passion for the lost in your life.

1. Cultivate Love for the Lost

We are surrounded by multitudes of lost souls whose eternal destiny is hell, and yet, mostly, we remain unmoved. So how do we cultivate love for the lost? We tend to think of love as a wave of emotion that suddenly possesses or overwhelms us, but the reverse is true. Love is cultivated over time.

We grow in love by noticing people, seeing their desirability to God, focusing on them and investing our time. Love between a man and a woman starts by them first noticing each other. After this they become aware of attractive characteristics in the other person. They may only see one or two small things to start with, but over time these traits can become more desirable and new traits are also discovered. They begin to focus more and more attention on each other, until an inner decision is made to invest greater amounts of time and resources into the other person.

This same progression is helpful in understanding how we can cultivate love for the lost. Firstly we have to notice them. They really exist and they are really headed for hell. Start looking at the people around you. As you notice them you will begin to see that each is uniquely and wonderfully made. Every individual is intensely desirable to God. Knowing this will cause you to focus your attention on them. Eventually your heart will become absorbed as you make an inner decision to invest more time, resources and energy in seeking and saving the lost.

Hope gives us a confident expectation that God will display His goodness to people through us. God does this by bringing understanding, conviction, repentance and salvation. Love compels us to action. As love increases so does faith. Paul says to the Galatians, 'Faith works by love' (Galatians 5:6). Faith releases God's supernatural power, which brings understanding, conviction, repentance and salvation.

2. Develop a Vision for Eternity

One of the main problems that faces the western church is apathy. But there is a solution. This solution does not primarily involve increased self-motivation. Self-motivation has more in common with our performance-based culture than it does with the Kingdom of God. Sometimes God has to wait until we have exhausted our own passion and zeal so that He can give us His. Whipping and beating ourselves or others into evangelism is not the answer. Apathy is caused by blindness. If our vision is dulled we have little to motivate and propel us towards God's eternal Kingdom.

Sadly, we live in an age that is not conducive to a vision of eternity. We have chosen to dwell on things that are immediate and temporal. But we need to remember that everything we do on earth has an impact on eternity. It is easy to waste time on essentially meaningless pursuits that have no eternal value. If we lived our whole lives in the light of eternity, we would live quite differently. Paul says in 2 Corinthians 4:17-18:

> For our light affliction, which is but for a moment, is working for us a far more exceeding and eternal weight of glory, while we do not look at the things which are seen, but at the things which are not seen. For the things which are seen are temporary, but the things which are not seen are eternal.

Paul's 'light affliction' which was 'but for a moment' is described a few verses earlier:

> We are hard pressed on every side, yet not crushed; we are perplexed, but not in despair; persecuted, but not forsaken; struck down, but not

destroyed – always carrying about in the body the dying of the Lord Jesus, that the life of Jesus also may be manifested in our body. For we who live are always delivered to death for Jesus' sake, that the life of Jesus also may be manifested in our mortal flesh (2 Corinthians 4:8-11).

For Paul eternal reality was much more important than temporal reality:

Therefore we make it our aim, whether present or absent, to be well pleasing to Him. For we must all appear before the judgment seat of Christ, that each one may receive the things done in the body, according to what he has done, whether good or bad. Knowing, therefore, the terror of the Lord, we persuade men (2 Corinthians 5:9-11a).

Paul's understanding of eternity and the terror of the Lord caused him to persuade men. If we do not live our own lives in the light of eternity, then naturally we will give little concern to those who are headed toward eternal damnation. C. S. Lewis aptly used the term 'shadowlands' when describing the temporal realm in which we live. Everything on earth is merely a shadow of that which is to come. When men and women leave this life and look back from either heaven or hell, it will be abundantly clear that this life was only a shadow. Heaven is more real and more wonderful than we can comprehend. Likewise, hell is both more real and more dreadful than we can comprehend.

A cursory study of hell in the scriptures is enough to send shivers down your spine. The Scriptures reveal that hell is a place where:

1. You are eternally separated from God
2. Fallen angels and humans dwell
3. You go by making a choice to reject and despise God
4. You increasingly reap for all eternity what you sow to the flesh while on earth
5. You are imprisoned in ever increasing loneliness, literally in hellish isolation
6. The only unity is a unity of fear

7. You are always reaching for something but never obtaining it

Hell is also a place of:

1. Unclean desire
2. Fiery torment so intense that even if you dwelt there you would do anything to prevent someone else from coming
3. Great regret
4. Intense gnawing emptiness
5. Falsity – everything is unreal

When the English criminal Charlie Peace was being taken to his execution, a chaplain was unemotionally reading aloud from prepared passages of scripture. Charlie stopped the man and said, 'Excuse me, Mister Chaplain. Where are you reading from?'

The Chaplain replied, 'The Bible.'

Charlie continued, 'Do you believe it?'

'Yes,' said the Chaplin.

But Charlie was not satisfied, 'Do you really believe it?'

'Yes,' came the Chaplin's confident reply.

Finally Charlie pressed his point home by saying, 'Mister Chaplain, sir, if I believed what you and many Christians claim to believe, even one tenth of what you claim to believe about hell, I would crawl across England on my hands and knees, even if it were to be littered with glass pieces, and count it worth my while to save one soul from that hell that you so glibly talk about.'

The great evangelist and preacher Dwight L. Moody once said, 'When we preach on hell, we might at least do it with tears in our eyes.' It is said that he never preached on the doctrine of hell without breaking down in the middle of the sermon and weeping because of the enormous implications of what he was saying.

One time when I was holding meetings in a village in Vanuatu, God showed a teenage girl a vision of hell. It was so abhorrent to her that she was half shouting, half screaming, 'NO!!!' because she didn't want to see what she was seeing. How much differently would you and I live if we were to have just one glimpse of hell? As Leonard Ravenhill has said, 'Could a mariner sit idle if he heard the drowning cry? Could a doctor sit in comfort and let his patients die? Could a fireman sit idle, let men burn and give no hand? Can you sit at ease in Zion with the world around you damned?'

I fear that most of us have forgotten about eternity, subtly lulled to sleep by the spirit of the world and 'Christian' activity. One day we will all awake from this shadowland to stand before God. Everything about our life will be revealed by fire. 'For no other foundation can anyone lay than that which is laid, which is Jesus Christ. Now if anyone builds on this foundation with gold, silver, precious stones, wood, hay, straw, each one's work will become clear; for the Day will declare it, because it will be revealed by fire; and the fire will test each one's work, of what sort it is. If anyone's work which he has built on it endures, he will receive a reward. If anyone's work is burned, he will suffer loss; but he himself will be saved, yet so as through fire' (1 Corinthians 3:11-15). Will you stand before Him with regret because you wasted your life on things that didn't count for eternity?

Imagine realizing that you could have obtained 'a far more exceeding and eternal weight of glory' but didn't. The solution is to live for eternity now. Ask God to reveal eternity to you. Ask Him to enable you to live in the light of what comes after this life.

3. Walk in True Authority

One of the things that made Jesus' ministry so powerful was His authority. People did not rave to one another about how loving He was, rather they marveled at how authoritative He was (Mark 1:27). Some people resist true authority and say that it is unloving. Often what they really mean by 'loving' is 'nice'. But being nice and being loving are not the same thing. Jesus demonstrated His love through His authority. With this in mind, let us consider Jesus' last words as recorded in the gospel of Matthew.

And Jesus came and spoke to them, saying, 'All authority has been given to Me in heaven and on earth. Go therefore and make disciples of all the nations, baptizing them in the name of the Father and of the Son and of the Holy Spirit, teaching them to observe all things that I have commanded you; and lo, I am with you always, even to the end of the age.' Amen (Matthew 28:18-20).

The theme of these verses is authority. I believe that this one observation alone has the potential to completely revolutionize our concept and understanding of evangelism. We are to go in *His* authority. All true authority is rooted and grounded in love. Before Jesus obtained all authority in heaven and earth through His death and resurrection, He was sent to earth because of His Father's love for the world (John 3:16).

Jesus obtained authority because He loved God and mankind. Jesus let the love of His Father for mankind compel Him to leave heaven and come to earth as a human being. In the same way, we need to be compelled by love, not compelled by compulsion. When we connect with the love of God and let it flow through us, we are compelled to go to the nations for His sake. Like Jesus, this process happens as we meet with the Father one to one. Jesus stepped into time propelled by the strength of an eternal relationship with His Father. Even as a human being, the fellowship that Jesus had with His Father was more important than anything else.

True authority comes out of loving truly. The more transparent, vulnerable and intimate our lives become toward God, the more authority we have. What should we do with this authority? Go and make disciples. Disciples are not 'converts' nor are they 'salvations'. The disciples of Jesus were those who had left everything else behind to follow Him and conform to His way of life. Jesus gave two instructions for making disciples:

1. *Baptize them in the name of the Father and of the Son and of the Holy Spirit.* The Greek word for baptize means to immerse completely. But it is speaking of an experience, not a formula. We are baptized *into* something or someone. Nowhere in this passage does it mention anything about water. I am not saying that Jesus is not referring to water baptism. What I am saying is that the emphasis is not on the physical act of water

baptism, as important as that is. The emphasis here is on being immersed *into* a dynamic relationship with the Father, the Son and the Holy Spirit.

Over the centuries so much emphasis has been given to the outward ritual and external compliance with God's command, that in many cases the true experience has been lost altogether. True disciples come to know the Father, the Son and the Holy Spirit as distinct persons. Although the Trinity is one, each member has a unique and distinctive personality.

Our relationship with the Father is like the relationship that a trusting child has with a loving natural father. Our relationship with Jesus is like that of a bride to a bridegroom. Our relationship with the Holy Spirit is like that of a close and intimate friend. He is the One who connects us with Jesus and the Father. Some people struggle to know who to address when they pray. Let me simply say that there is no jealousy in the Godhead. The prayers in the New Testament are addressed to God the Father. This in no way limits us to communicating only with Him. Jesus is the way to the Father and it is through the Holy Spirit that we have access to both the Father and the Son.

2. *Teach them to observe all things that Jesus commanded us to do.* There are two ways to teach: the first involves telling others what to do, the second involves training by example. Jesus used both methods, but primarily He trained by example. Teachers do not have true authority if their lifestyles contradict what they teach. Jesus' death on the cross was the most important example He gave His disciples. It was a summary of His entire life on earth. To teach others to observe all the things that Jesus commanded is to teach them to love as Jesus loved, even unto death. Jesus lived a life of sacrifice, and His disciples should do likewise. There are two questions we need to ask ourselves. Have we been making disciples or converts and pew-sitters? And, do we act in *His* authority?

Jesus concludes His teaching on earth by saying that He will be with us always. This means that His authority should rest with us always, even to the end of the age.

4. Follow Jesus

Jesus said, 'Follow Me, and I will make you fishers of men' (Matthew 4:19). Becoming a 'fisher of men' is a consequence of following Jesus. It is not something we do naturally by ourselves. It requires us to let Him make us into what *He* wants to make us. The natural consequence of following Him is that men, women and children are snatched from Satan's dominion and transported into God's eternal Kingdom.

Four of Jesus' twelve disciples were fishermen, and all these men were very close to Jesus.

> And Jesus, walking by the Sea of Galilee, saw two brothers, Simon called Peter, and Andrew his brother, casting a net into the sea; for they were fishermen. Then He said to them, 'Follow Me, and I will make you fishers of men.' They immediately left their nets and followed Him. Going on from there, He saw two other brothers, James the son of Zebedee, and John his brother, in the boat with Zebedee their father, mending their nets. He called them, and immediately they left the boat and their father, and followed Him (Matthew 4:18-22).

In Bible days, fishing was a team effort. With a line and a hook, one person can catch fish, but two or more people with a net can catch many more. Relationships are an important aspect of evangelism. Jesus said that our love for one another would be a witness to the world. God wants to build teams of people who will work together to bring others to Him. These teams will only be as strong as the relationships that tie them together.

Notice what these four fishermen had to leave behind in order to follow Jesus: their nets, their boats and their families. Jesus replaced these physical entities with spiritual equivalents.

Their nets. A net is representative of a network of relationships. Any gap in that net means that fish can swim through. Fishermen need to mend their nets continually. When Jesus' disciples became apostles, one of their most important tasks was to repair broken relationships. Like nets, relationships are most often broken in the places where there is the greatest pressure and strain. Repairing these relationships is vitally important and many will find themselves called to this ministry (2 Corinthians 5:18).

Their boats. Boats carry fishermen to the fish. In Scripture, the sea often symbolically represents the people of the world. 'Boats' can be seen as the vehicles that take us to these people. A ministry, church or outreach team could all be likened to boats.

It has become common to talk about 'taking the walls off the church'. This means reaching into the community and removing the things that keep the unsaved from coming to us. Criticism, judgment, selfishness, tradition, lack of vision and falsity are the kinds of things that can discourage people from coming into the church. In some cases, people have tried to win the lost by making the church more acceptable to the world, but this usually results in a watered-down version of the gospel. The church is called to be transformed into the image of Christ; that is the only way we can transform the world.

Catching fish requires some basic skills. It involves understanding the habits and ways of the fish and the sea, as well as a lot of patience and perseverance. Wise fishers of men always seek strategic revelation from God. Fishing involves throwing out the nets again and again. Jesus used two main analogies about evangelism: fishing, and growing and harvesting grain. Both of these examples involve the fisherman or farmer working in the same body of water or field repeatedly. Many churches give up after their initial efforts seem unfruitful. Grain is not harvested overnight, and people are not always instantly won to Jesus. Many hear the message of the gospel a number of times before it finds its way into their hearts. It is easy for evangelism to be motivated by our desire to build and grow a successful church rather than a genuine concern for the welfare of the lost, but people can tell if our motives are not genuine.

Their families. The third sacrifice that the disciples made was in leaving their families behind. Fishing was often a family business. Jesus' call to become fishers of men was a call to be part of a new family – the family of God. Jesus pointed His disciples to the Father – He was the way to the Father (John 14:6). Through Him they came to understand the Father's heart for all people (John 3:16). This gave them the motivation to become fishers of men.

When Peter stood up and preached on the day of Pentecost, 3000 people were saved. Although Peter was the main spokesman, it was a team effort that led to that result. One hundred and twenty believers were gathered in the upper room when the Holy Spirit came, and they all played a significant part in subsequent events.

Although Peter, Andrew, James and John had to leave behind things that were an integral part of their lives as fishermen, in exchange Jesus equipped them with tools that enabled them to become effective fishers of men.

At the beginning of this book I told the story of how the face of Jesus appeared to myself and others (including twenty-one children) in Port Vila, Vanuatu. During this time one of the boys had a vision of their pastor casting a large fishing net, and of the children chasing fish into that net.

The children performed their dances at the nightly crusade meetings. As is the custom for crusade meetings in Vanuatu, many groups did items, but the dances that the children performed were by far the most interesting and anointed. As soon as it was their turn to perform, it was as if everybody in the large crowd suddenly woke up and paid attention. At the one altar call given during the crusade meetings thirty families came forward for salvation.

Corporate evangelism like this is very powerful, exhilarating and exciting. It has the potential to change whole nations. God is calling His Church to cast out huge nets to bring in the catch. It will involve great faith, courage, dedication and sacrifice. Satan knows that if we advance together with faith and determination his work will be destroyed, so he works overtime to keep us from being joined corporately.

Passion is *caught* more than it is *taught*. It can be hard to summon up passion as an individual, but when God moves on His Church as a unified body, passion becomes explosive. God wants to give us *His* passion for the lost.

Part 5:

ENTERING GOD'S EMBRACE

THE STORY OF GOD & MANKIND

The greatest stories usually involve the fulfillment of a cherished dream despite great suffering and overwhelming odds. Passion is shown to be enduring when it has been given ample opportunity to die, and yet still lives on. The greatest story of all time is the story of God and humankind. It is a story that is still being written in the lives of multitudes of men and women today. Each individual life is just one thread that is being carefully woven into this epic. The story of God and mankind is both tragic and triumphant. The tragedy lies in the fact that our free choice has the power to deny God the passion of His heart. The triumph is in God finding people of passion in the midst of a world given over to rebellion. God's cry is expressed in the words of this song by Kent Henry:

> Where are the people of passion?
> Where are the people who care?
> Where are those who will steal away, find God in the secret lair?
>
> Where are the people of fire?
> Where are the people of zeal?
> Where are those with a Jesus heart and hands that really heal?

The song continues in response to the above questions:

> We are the people, people of holiness.
> We are the people, people of righteousness.
> We are the people, people of zeal and fire.
> We are the people, people of God's desire.

We are the people with minstrel hearts.
We are the people of song.
We are those with the psalmist voice, singing the Father's song.

We are the people of Heaven's grace.
We are the people who share,
His passion and zeal to touch the world, displaying His holy care.[1]

Passion is either contagious or controversial. For those who are bored with a Christianity that is apathetic and lukewarm, passion is contagious. For those who want everything to stay the same, passion is viewed as dangerous, and controversy usually erupts. The more intense the passion, the more intense the controversy.

Toward the end of his life, the apostle John was shown an open door into heaven. As he looked at the door a strong voice called him up to go through it. Immediately John found himself in the spirit before the throne of God. The One who sat on the throne had a scroll in His hand but there was no one in heaven, on earth, or under the earth that could open the scroll. John wept because of this situation, but was told to stop weeping because the Lion of the Tribe of Judah was able to open the scroll. When John looked up, he did not see a Lion but a Lamb, and the Lamb appeared to have been slain. The slain Lamb was able to remove the seals and open the scroll.

John was called up into the heavens to receive a fuller revelation of the cross of Christ. He had already witnessed the crucifixion of Jesus first-hand. The startling and cataclysmic events that are revealed to John in the remainder of the book of Revelation are a direct result of the cross of Christ. These events climax in the Bride of Christ making herself ready for Him (Revelation 19:7).

Even now God wants us to see the open door into heaven. He is calling us to come through that door and see the Lamb who was slain. This revelation will empower the end-time Church. God is looking for people with the same fervency of love that led Jesus to die on the cross. We can become an extension of the Father's heart, making *His* passions, *His* desires, *His* zeal and *His* fire our own.

The Message of the Cross

The central message of Christianity is Christ and His cross. Paul said that he was determined to know nothing among the Corinthians except Christ and Him crucified.

> And I, brethren, when I came to you, did not come with excellence of speech or of wisdom declaring to you the testimony of God. For I determined not to know anything among you except Jesus Christ and Him crucified. I was with you in weakness, in fear, and in much trembling. And my speech and my preaching were not with persuasive words of human wisdom, but in demonstration of the Spirit and of power, that your faith should not be in the wisdom of men but in the power of God (1 Corinthians 2:1-5).

Have we lost this message? William Booth, founder of the Salvation Army, spoke prophetically when he said, 'The chief danger of the 20th century will be religion without the Holy Ghost, Christianity without Christ, forgiveness without repentance, salvation without regeneration, and heaven without hell.' When Paul said, 'I preach Christ and Him crucified', he was not saying that he merely spoke *about* Christ and His crucifixion. Paul's preaching came with revelation and power, leaving the listener with an experiential understanding of who Christ is and what His crucifixion accomplished. Paul was not released into his God-given ministry until Christ was revealed *to* him and *in* him (Galatians 1:16). He was able to say, 'I have been crucified with Christ; it is no longer I who live, but Christ lives in me; and the life which I now live in the flesh I live by faith in the Son of God, who loved me and gave Himself for me' (Galatians 2:20).

The message of the cross will only be powerful if it is preached and demonstrated by those who are in the face of Christ and who take up their crosses daily. Paul died to his own desires, ambitions, thoughts and plans every day (1 Corinthians 15:31). The revelation of Christ and the cross will ignite passion like nothing else, and it is with good reason that the week that led up to Christ's crucifixion is known as 'passion week'.

The cross not only demonstrates the way to live the Christian life, it also gives us the means. By taking up our crosses daily, our flesh is crucified. Jesus' death was our death. We appropriate it by putting our faith in what was accomplished on the cross. If we are crucified with Him, we are also resurrected into a new life. Our cross is the circumstances that we face daily, circumstances that allow us to choose either *our* life and *our* own response, or *His* life and *His* way of responding. Consider this: the cross is where God's will and your will cross. The cross is also where your will and the will of others cross.

God is calling us into a revelation of the cross of Christ that will ignite fiery passion for the Son of God. Those who embrace and receive this revelation will be part of the new breed that God is summoning in our time.

The Two Sides of the Cross

There are two sides to the cross that we need to embrace: the mercy and the justice of God. The foundations of God's throne are righteousness and justice. When we approach His throne we are overwhelmed by His mercy and grace – mercy that triumphs over judgment, and grace that empowers us to overcome sin and live in righteousness.

Criticism and judgment drive people away, whereas mercy and grace draw them closer. If we have devoted ourselves to God, our lives will be built on the foundations of righteousness and justice, but they will exude the fragrance of mercy and grace.

Sinners were drawn to Jesus, not repelled by Him. Those who felt like they were not making it, or felt like they never could make it, were totally accepted in His presence. Jesus inspired hope in the hopeless. A short time with Him could turn unbelief into faith and hatred into love. 'For the law was given through Moses, but grace and truth came through Jesus Christ' (John 1:17). As we come to God's throne, we too will find ourselves full of grace and truth.

It is interesting to consider the example David left us. With the exception of Jesus, more is written about David than any other man in Scripture. The psalms that he wrote reveal that he had a deep understanding of the character and nature of God. David was a man who embraced the passions of God's heart and made them his own. He also made a lot of mistakes in his life, and yet the final verdict on his life was that he was a man after God's own heart. God saw the desire and intent of David's heart and judged him accordingly, despite his failings. Above all else, he wanted to please God and was deeply grieved at how his sin had wounded God's heart.

How is it that after committing adultery and murder, David was still able to carry on as Israel's king? David understood the mercy of God better than most. He was in touch with the depth of the human heart and allowed God to search him at that level. David also had an insatiable longing to know God's heart, not only God's joy and delight but also His grief, sorrow, pain and suffering. He was utterly dependent on the mercy and kindness of God, and knew that even though God is a God of justice, His mercies never fail.

Paul, like David, was a man who sought to know God's heart above everything else. One of Paul's most heartfelt prayers was to know the fellowship of Christ's suffering (Philippians 3:10). By our own foolishness and pride, we bring a lot of suffering on ourselves. But the fellowship of Christ's suffering is when God orchestrates circumstances to bring us into a greater understanding of the cross of Christ. You might currently be in such a place. Many people have an understanding of the provision of the cross without going on to know the fellowship of Christ's suffering.

Those who seek God with their whole hearts will find themselves in circumstances that He uses to teach them the way of the cross. However, the fellowship of Christ's suffering is more than just circumstances. David experienced the fellowship of Christ's suffering even before the historical event of Christ's crucifixion (for example Psalm 22). And it is interesting to note that like Christ, Paul died having been betrayed and abandoned by some of his close friends. In the simplest terms the way of the cross is forgiveness.

Where are the people of passion? The truth is that many of them actually feel completely passionless. But through their times of trial and barrenness, they are learning the ways of the cross and are entering into a greater revelation of it. The time will come when they will be used to reveal the fiery love of God's heart to a world that is estranged from Him and crying out to know true love. Consumed with passion for Him, they will preach Christ and His cross. This will result in a restoration of the dominion that was taken by the Serpent from Adam and Eve (Colossians 2:15).

Dominion and Fruitfulness

After God created Adam and Eve, He gave them a mandate to have dominion over all the earth (Genesis 1:26-30). Their authority for dominion was taken from them by the Serpent. But the Bride of Christ is being prepared to retake that dominion. Adam and Eve lost their authority by choosing to sin. But the Bride of Christ will gain authority by choosing to overcome sin. We are being prepared to rule with Christ for eternity. Passion and fire for the Son of God is about entering into our ultimate destiny as His Bride. That process goes something like this: attraction, courtship, covenant, intimacy, dominion.

Not only are we being prepared to take dominion, we are also being prepared for fruitfulness. God's command to Adam and Eve was to be fruitful and multiply. This fruitfulness will take place in the future, but through our relationship with Christ we are also called to be fruitful now (Matthew 28:18-20, Luke 10:19, John 15:4-5).

Abraham and Sarah

Abraham and Sarah were unable to have children because Sarah was barren. They were also well past the age of child-bearing. But God promised Abraham that he would have a son with Sarah. Abraham was 75 years old when he received this promise. For 25 years he and Sarah waited. 'And the Lord visited Sarah as He had said, and the Lord did for Sarah as He had spoken. For Sarah conceived and bore Abraham a son in his old age, at the set time of which God had spoken to him' (Genesis 21:1-2).

Sarah became pregnant only after God visited her. In a similar way, God wants to visit us and make us 'pregnant' with His promise. This brings us to an important point. Many Christians want to be wooed into a covenant relationship but they do not want to give themselves over completely to God. It is as if they don't mind being courted but try to protect themselves against commitment and the conception of His will. As a result they are unfruitful. God calls us to 'give birth' to His purposes on the earth. Passion and fire must lead to conception. In this case, the process goes like this: attraction, courtship, commitment (covenant relationship), intimacy, conception, gestation, travail, fruitfulness.

Harem or Bridal Chamber?

My definition of intercession is: knowing the heartbeat of God and joining with Him to make it happen. Fruitfulness comes as a result of abiding in Christ. It is impossible to give birth to God's purposes in our own strength. People can intercede all they like, but unless there is first a conception (when God gives His will to us) nothing will be accomplished. Travail does not happen because we decide that it will. It happens because what has been conceived in us has reached the proper phase of maturity.

Many times the spiritual seeds that God puts in the Church die there. It is not 'convenient' to give birth. But a mother goes through the inconvenience of carrying her developing child and the pain of childbirth because of the joy of what's to come. We must guard the seeds that God plants in our hearts and hold onto the vision of what God will accomplish in the right season. 'Where there is no revelation [or as the KJV says, 'vision'], the people cast off restraint' (Proverbs 29:18 – brackets mine).

Conception comes from intimacy and faithfulness to God. 'Adulterers and adulteresses!' James thundered, 'Do you not know that friendship with the world is enmity with God? Whoever therefore wants to be a friend of the world makes himself an enemy of God' (James 4:4). God wants a bride, not a harem. Harems are based on relationships of convenience. But bridal chambers are places where the destinies of two become one. That is the story of God and mankind.

Entwined Forever

There is no greater romance than the eternal romance that will exist between Christ and His Bride. Consider the following Scriptures.

Paul to the Ephesians:

Husbands, love your wives, just as Christ also loved the church and gave Himself for her, that He might sanctify and cleanse her with the washing of water by the word, that He might present her to Himself a glorious church, not having spot or wrinkle or any such thing, but that she should be holy and without blemish. So husbands ought to love their own wives as their own bodies; he who loves his wife loves himself.

For no one ever hated his own flesh, but nourishes and cherishes it, just as the Lord does the church. For we are members of His body, of His flesh and of His bones.

'For this reason a man shall leave his father and mother and be joined to his wife, and the two shall become one flesh.' This is a great mystery, but I speak concerning Christ and the church (Ephesians 5:25-32).

Jesus to His disciples:

I do not pray for these alone, but also for those who will believe in Me through their word; that they all may be one, as You, Father, are in Me, and I in You; that they also may be one in Us, that the world may believe that You sent Me. And the glory which You gave Me I have given them, that they may be one just as We are one: I in them, and You in Me; that they may be made perfect in one, and that the world may know that You have sent Me, and have loved them as You have loved Me (John 17:20-23).

Paul to the Corinthians:

For I am jealous for you with godly jealousy. For I have betrothed you to one husband, that I may present you as a chaste virgin to Christ (2 Corinthians 11:3).

The Revelation given to John:

And I heard, as it were, the voice of a great multitude, as the sound of many waters and as the sound of mighty thunderings, saying, 'Alleluia! For the Lord God Omnipotent reigns! Let us be glad and rejoice and give Him glory, for the marriage of the Lamb has come, and His wife has made herself ready.' And to her it was granted to be arrayed in fine linen, clean and bright, for the fine linen is the righteous acts of the saints. Then he said to me, 'Write: "Blessed are those who are called to the marriage supper of the Lamb!"' And he said to me, 'These are the true sayings of God' (Revelation 19:6-9).

It is significant to note that the Bible begins and ends with a marriage.

And the Lord God caused a deep sleep to fall on Adam, and he slept; and He took one of his ribs, and closed up the flesh in its place. Then the rib which the Lord God had taken from man He made into a woman, and He brought her to the man. And Adam said: 'This is now bone of my bones and flesh of my flesh; she shall be called Woman, because she was taken out of Man.' Therefore a man shall leave his father and mother and be joined to his wife, and they shall become one flesh. And they were both naked, the man and his wife, and were not ashamed (Genesis 2:21-25).

Adam and Eve enjoyed a relationship of unbroken fellowship with each other. In this relationship they were totally transparent and experienced no shame. After sin entered the world, this state of bliss was shattered. The rest of the Bible is the story of God's plan for the redemption of humankind.

In the future there will once again be a marriage unmarred by sin; this time it will be between Christ and the Church. Eve made a choice to sin even though she lived in a perfect environment. Those who become part of Christ's Bride will have done so by their own choice to overcome sin in an environment corrupted by its power – 'the bride has made *herself* ready'.

In the beginning, God made Eve as a companion for Adam. God did this supernatural act by putting Adam into a deep sleep and making Eve from Adam's rib. The story of Eve's creation, although literal, also reads as an allegory of Christ and His Bride. God was not lonely and in need of someone to keep Him company. But His creation was not complete until He had someone to share it with, someone comparable to Him – figuratively speaking, 'bone of his bones and flesh of his flesh'. Eve came out of Adam's side (the Hebrew word translated 'rib' can also be translated 'side'), and blood and water flowed from the side of Christ on the cross (John 19:34). Through that blood, a Bride will come forth made up of people from every nation. Just as Eve came from inside Adam, Christ's Bride will come from inside Him. 'And they sang a new song, saying: "You are worthy to take the scroll, and to open its seals; for You were slain, and have redeemed us to God by Your blood out of every tribe and tongue and people and nation, and have made us kings and priests to our God; and we shall reign on the earth"' (Revelation 5:9-10).

When the Spirit and the Bride are one in purpose and heart, a unified cry will be heard in the heavens to beckon the heavenly Bridegroom to come for His long awaited Bride. 'And the Spirit and the bride say, "Come!" And let him who hears say, "Come!"' (Revelation 22:17).

The Bride is making herself ready. Her cry is the cry of Song of Solomon 8:6-7. 'Set me as a seal upon your heart, as a seal upon your arm; for love is as strong as death, jealousy as cruel as the grave; its flames are flames of fire, a most vehement flame. Many waters cannot quench love, nor can the floods drown it. If a man would give for love all the wealth of his house, it would be utterly despised.'

This life is the dressing room for the greatest marriage of all. Now is the time to prepare. Now is the time to leave behind mediocrity and encounter the passion and fire of God's heart. The Bride has embarked on a passionate quest – a quest that is energized by the simple truth that God has first loved her.

EPILOGUE

After reaching the top of the mountains it became my joy and delight to make the journey again and again. The warmth of the sun, the clear mountain air, the rugged terrain and the beauty of the land below brought me rest and peace. But by far the greatest pleasure was meeting with God face to face. Every time I saw Him, I became more consumed with His passion. The people in the village below were more precious to Him than I could ever comprehend.

As I looked at the people, a dramatic picture opened up before my eyes. I saw the village suspended in space – almost as if it hung between heaven and earth. The Father's affection for the villagers was so great that when He looked at them everything else disappeared. He reached out and cupped the whole village in the palm of His hand.

As I watched, I could faintly hear a voice crying out in longing and grief. The sound rose and fell like the swells of an ocean. I was reminded of Solomon's words about Wisdom crying out in every public and prominent place (Proverbs 8:1-5), and of Jeremiah's words about Rachel's lamentation for her children (Jeremiah 31:15). Was I hearing the heart of the Father?

As the Father continued to gaze lovingly at the people, a single teardrop fell from His eye and spread out across the entire village. The instant this happened the volume and intensity of the voice increased. The villagers responded in various ways. Those who had heard the initial cry of the voice, faint as it was, began to listen more intently, some of them even fell to their knees and hid their faces. Another group of people began to hear the voice for the first time. Some listened momentarily and then carried on as if nothing had changed. Some appeared frightened by the voice and busied themselves with activity in an attempt to drown out the persistent cry. A few began to listen more intently.

The combination of the Father's tear and the increase in the voice caused the village to start shaking. For those who were listening, the shaking started with a tremble inside their own hearts. Powerful love began to erupt everywhere. As the shaking continued, many of the edifices and structures in the village began to change. Only the things that bore the image of Christ were left standing. There was confusion as the face and shape of the village was altered, but I knew that the shaking was necessary. It was the Father's desire to remove everything that stood in the way of the expression of love between His Son and those who were being prepared as the Bride.

As these things were removed, I saw a map of the whole world superimposed over the village as the Father stirred up passion in the village for all nations.

Then I saw the Father turn towards Jesus, the Bridegroom. With determination and joy the Father offered the village and the nations of the earth as a gift to Him. And as He did, the people began to burn with divine love.

The vision faded but I continued to tremble. Not only was my heart on fire, it was filled with awe and anticipation. Now I knew that many in the village were about to be awakened to the passion and fire of God's heart. Many would venture beyond their confines to discover the beauty and the majesty of the mountains.

God gives an invitation for each one of us to make the journey. May the blazing fire of His love awaken you. May it capture you. May it set you free from the ordinary, the mundane and the temporal. May you rest in His fiery love, revel in His indescribable beauty, delight in the warmth of His embrace and pursue Him with every atom and fibre of your being. As His Bride you will not be satisfied until you are *completely* in His embrace – entwined forever.

NOTES

The Baptism of Fire

1. Strong's Hebrew Dictionary – 5475.
2. Breathe by Marie Barnett © 1995 Mercy/Vineyard Publishing.
3. Vines – Know.
4. Discovery Bible – Know.
5. Poem from Shake Off The Dust © 1999 Howling Prairie Music.

The Secret Place

1. There Must Be A Place by Brian Doerken, Paul Janz, Daphne Rademaker © 1994 Father's House Publishing/All That Janz/East Broadway Music. Administered by Mercy/Vineyard Publishing.
2. Strong's Greek Dictionary – 3306.

The Great Deception

1. Earwicker, Evan. Dance With Me © 2002 Unseen Obsession Music.
2. Let Me Burn by Andrew Smith © 1999 Howling Prairie Music.
3. Joyner, Rick. The Final Quest. MorningStar Publications.
4. I highly recommend reading the section on 'How We See God' from John and Paula Sandford's book *The Transformation of the Inner Man*, as well as the minibook *Betrayed!* which can be obtained through Heart of David Ministries.
5. His Love by David Ruis © 1993 Mercy/Vineyard Publishing.

Emotions: Expressed or Stifled

1. Strong's Greek Dictionary – 2705.

The Father's Desire

1. *The Way of the Master* book and DVDs available from www.livingwaters.com in the United States and www.livingwatersnewzealand.com in New Zealand.

Igniting Passion for the Lost

1. The Morning Star Journal Volume 3 Number 3.

The Story of God and Mankind

1. People of Passion by Kent Henry © 1991 Kent Henry Ministries.

ABOUT THE AUTHOR

Nathan Shaw has been involved in active ministry for over 18 years, working in over 10 different nations. He has a passion to see people encounter God through the Holy Spirit and to experience the holiness and love of the Father. He is the founder of Heart of David Ministries and the pastor and founder of Fire and Destiny Centre in Dunedin, New Zealand.

Passion and Fire is his second book. His first book, *Unto the Least of These*, communicates God's heart for widows, divorcees and the fatherless.

Free audio messages by Nathan are available for download on www.heartofdavidministries.org and www.fireanddestiny.org.

ALSO BY NATHAN SHAW

Unto the Least of These: Expressing God's Love to Widows and the Fatherless

Widows, divorcees and the fatherless are some of the loneliest people on earth.

Nathan Shaw has a heart for this disenfranchised portion of Christ's Church and presents healing words to those who are brokenhearted. He issues a challenge for all Christians to mirror the Father's heart to those who are hurting and vulnerable.

"Nathan makes us painfully aware how we have not only not succored widows and orphans, but we have actually increased their sufferings by our judgments, both expressed and undercurrent."
– John Loren Sandford, Elijah House

"A clarion call for us to draw near to God and let His concern become our concern... a cutting edge message for the twenty-first century."
– Mike Bickle, International House of Prayer

Order online at www.heartofdavidministries.com
Also available from Castle Publishing orders@castlepublishing.co.nz

www.ingramcontent.com/pod-product-compliance
Lightning Source LLC
Chambersburg PA
CBHW020652300426
44112CB00007B/354